HOW TO MEASURE AND REPORT INNOVATION PERFORMANCE IN COMPANIES

Using Four Metrics

HOW TO MEASURE AND REPORT INNOVATION PERFORMANCE IN COMPANIES

Using Four Metrics

DAVID MASUMBA

Printed in the United States of America

Publisher: KDP

ISBN Paperback: 978-1-7341913-6-3

ISBN eBook: 978-1-7341913-7-0

Beloved wife Mujjna, daughter Waana and son Luwi

CONTENTS

PREFACE

"What we measure informs what we do.
And if we're measuring the wrong thing, we're going to do the wrong thing."

—Joseph Stiglitz, Nobel Prize Winner

Innovation is now one of the most critical factors for the success of the organization. However, to become a truly innovation-led company and accruing meaningful benefits involves cultivating innovation across all the functional units of the organization by implementing innovation-related strategies, policies and activities. This involves a lot of moving parts. One of the innovation practices that is key to cultivating innovation and high possibility for accruing meaningful benefits is implementing a company-wide mechanism for measuring and reporting innovation performance.

My experience with companies and studies show that many companies struggle with measuring and reporting innovation across functional units. This book aims to provide tools to help managers build essential skills and knowledge for measuring and reporting innovation performance in organizations.

INTRODUCTION

Story of the Island of Nada

We have used the short story of a fictitious country, the Republic of Nada, to kickstart the introduction to this book.

The Republic of Nada is an island country located 400 miles off the Eastern coast of Africa. The Island is 4,700 square kilometres big. Since 2005, the government of the Island of Nada has pursued robust market-oriented economic policies. Below is a sketch map of the Republic of Nada.

As a result of the good free-market economic policies and robust and diverse infrastructure development projects implemented by the government, the country has enjoyed a booming tourism industry, which is the mainstay of the country's economy. The total economic contribution of the tourism industry is about 60% of the country's Gross Domestic Product (GDP). In terms of employment, tourism is the catalyst for about 55% of the country's employment base (direct and indirect). Other industries include livestock and crop export. Smaller industries include light manufacturing, financial, and insurances services. Since 2010, the country's standard of living has increased, and the country has since graduated from Middle Income Country (MIC) to High Income Country (HIC).

Like any other country around the globe, the Covid-19 pandemic has had a significant impact on the tourism industry of the Republic of Nada due to travel restrictions as well as a slump in demand by travellers. It is common knowledge that, globally, the tourism industry has been massively affected by the spread of Covid-19 since many countries have implemented travel restrictions to contain the spread of the virus. According to the United Nations Tourism Organization, the global international tourist might decrease by 20-30% in 2020. In Kezhi, for instance, the island's top tourist destination, foreign arrivals fell by 98%—four months into the Covid-19 pandemic.

It's been three months since the Nada government began lifting restrictions and reopening of the country's economic and social activities. Like everyone in the country, government leaders are eager to see economic activities return to optimal operations, but things are not moving at a desired speed, despite the country-wide infection rate of the coronavirus being at very low levels.

Economic Diversification

With the tourism sector reeling from the impact of the coronavirus, the country's economy has shrunk by a whopping 10 % by June 2020. The government has therefore prioritized a raft of measures to facilitate a rebound of the economy post-Covid. Most of the measures are also aimed at building the country's economic resilience capabilities to withstand future economic global crises.

So, on October 30, 2020, the President of the Republic of Nada launched the country's Vision 2025. The main aim of the national vision is to diversify the nation's economy beyond tourism and also build an innovation-led economy. In its diversification vision, the government is seeking to reduce overdependence on tourism by expanding portfolios of export goods and, also, diversifying service sectors. The government's goal is to reduce dependence on earnings from tourism by at least 20% by 2025.

Innovation is the Key Ingredient

The government of Nada understands that for the country to achieve its economic diversification goals and realize the country's Vision 2025, there are two factors:

- Innovation will be a key ingredient.
- Scaling innovation across sectors will not happen naturally. It will occur only if innovation-support capabilities and programs are developed by both public institutions and private sector organizations.

Based on these two factors, the government of Nada is championing innovation across sectors by building and promoting required linkages for driving innovation.

Formation of National Innovation Linkages

As a way of championing institutionalized innovation across sectors, the Nada government has established the National Innovation Empowerment Agency (NIEA), whose focus is to foster innovation across all sectors of the country's economy and public service delivery. In order to fulfil its mandate, the NIEA has launched the National Innovation System (NIS) which will be used as a vehicle to champion innovation performance by promoting the formulation of innovation systems and strategies across all key sectors and industries of the Nada economy.

What is a national innovation system? *It is a network of relationships, interactions, and initiatives among private and public sectors (including professional associations, industry associations, tertiary, and government institutions aimed at contributing toward advancing innovation across sectors).* For the government of Nada, a national innovation system means that all stakeholders, especially in the private sector, in the country are expected to contribute toward developing support systems that will advance innovation in their respective sectors.

Innovation Skills Development Programs by Nada Chamber of Commerce and Industry

The Nada Chamber of Commerce and Industry (NCCI) has identified initiatives and approaches to contribute toward advancing innovation in member companies. One such initiative is to help companies develop frameworks for measuring and reporting innovation performance. By doing so, the NCCI and its members will be contributing toward realizing the country's vision of developing an innovation-led economy. Since innovation is a business and economic strategy that cannot be driven without metrics, an initiative to help companies measure and report innovation performance is a vital and welcome move.

DM Personal Care Products Enterprises

A fictitious company, DM Personal Care Products Enterprises is one of the few manufacturing companies on the Island of Nada. The company manufactures a variety of personal care products. Sensing a huge opportunity in creating an innovation-led company and potentially benefitting meaningfully from innovation to drive growth, the company's top leadership wants to get ahead of the pack in championing and implementing innovation practices such as innovation measurement. The company's leadership has commissioned a taskforce to help each functional unit across the company develop a tool for measuring and reporting innovation performance.

Let's assume the company has the following functional units:

Core units

- Product development unit with the following segments:
  - Body lotions segment
  - Skin cleansing segment
  - Hair care segment
  - Hand washing segment
- Manufacturing processes department (the manufacturing processes department comprises the same segments as the product development unit)
- Marketing department with the following units:
  - Pricing unit
  - Product promotion unit
  - Product delivery unit
  - New markets unit
  - Packaging unit
- Customer service department

Support units

- Procurement
- HR
- Finance and accounting
- IT
- Corporate affairs

About this Book

Although this book has used the fictitious country, Republic of Nada, as a basis to kickstart the introduction, the challenges of measuring innovation performance in companies run deep across industries.

When I conduct training on measuring innovation performance, I sometimes ask delegates to indicate by a show of hands if their companies have policies for reporting innovation performance at the functional-unit level, divisional level, or corporate level. I have never gotten more than five "yes" hands out of a group of, say, twenty-five to forty. Interestingly, when I ask the delegates to indicate whether innovation is considered a top-three priority in their organizations, 90–95 percent of the delegates raise their hands. Not long ago, innovation in organizations was perceived as the responsibility of specific functional units and professionals. That's no longer the case; study after study has revealed that many organizations now perceive innovation as everyone's job, from senior leadership to the most junior employee. This book contests that in order to make innovation everyone's job, organizational leaders need to implement a raft of innovation support programs and interventions. One such intervention is measuring innovation performance across functional units. In other words, a company cannot sustain a culture of innovation without an effective mechanism for tracking and measuring innovation performance across functional units. However, as stated earlier, measuring innovation performance seems to be huge challenge with many companies.

According to a study by McKinsey & Company, more than 70 percent of corporate leaders tout innovation as a top three priority, but only 22 percent set innovation metrics. An innovation survey by the Boston Consulting Group, a US-based consulting firm, revealed that although 73 percent of companies surveyed across the globe believe that innovation performance should be tracked as rigorously as other business elements, only 46 percent of the executives said their companies actually track innovation performance. And in a 2011 survey of more than six hundred executives worldwide by the US-based Institute for Corporate Productivity, many respondents indicated that one of the challenges they were wrestling with was how to measure and report the innovation performance of their organizations. Because of the difficulties that many managers face in measuring and reporting the innovation performance of their organizations, this book has provided tools to help organizational leaders build the essential skills and knowledge for measuring and reporting innovation performance across functional units. This book suggests a model aimed at helping organizations determine if their investments in innovation support programs are productive based on the four metrics of innovation performance measurement.

Definition of Innovation Concepts

By its nature, measuring of innovation performance in a company is not easy. But it is even harder for the leadership to adopt innovation performance measurement if the organizational leaders do not understand the vital concepts related to innovation. For this reason, it's important to ensure that the leadership understands the meaning of the three vital innovation concepts and how the meaning relates to the organization's business model and functional units.

- Innovation
- Dimensions of Innovation
- Innovation Performance Measurement

Innovation

This book defines 'innovation' as: *a process that involves identifying a problem or need, generating a new idea that has not been seen on the market before, turning the idea into a solution to address the identified need, then converting the solution into monetary value.*

Chapter Nine of my book, *Leadership for Innovation* describes in detail how to translate the meaning of innovation in the context of the company's functional activities and business model.

Dimensions of Innovation

Innovation occurs in different organizational contexts, and these contexts are what we've referred to as dimensions of innovation. The term *dimensions of innovation* refers to ways in which innovation occurs in the context of an organization's functional units and business model. In other words, because innovation occurs in different contexts of organizational activities, *dimensions of innovation* is a term that describes the different ways in which innovation occurs (i.e., *where*) and the degree of change or newness that innovation entails (i.e., *how*). In a nutshell, *dimensions of innovation* is a term that describes two related innovation concepts: *types of innovation* and *innovation degree*. Understanding the *dimensionality of innovation* is vital when it comes to measuring and reporting innovation performance across functional units.

Types of Innovation

The term *types of innovation* relates to where innovation occurs or the context in which innovation occurs in the organization's value chain or functional activities. Innovation occurs in a variety of functional activities across the organization's value chain. Examples of types of innovation include: product innovations, service innovations, process innovations, marketing innovations, and customer service innovations, etc. Types of innovation can be broadened to specifically reflect the organization's functional activities and business model. Chapter Nine of the *Leadership for Innovation* (2020), describes in detail how to translate types of innovation in the context of the company's functional activities and business model.

Innovations Implemented in Support Functional Units

You will notice that this book has included reporting innovation performance in support functional units. It is important to understand that that in addition to the innovations that are generated in the organization's core functional units, there are also types of innovations aimed at back-office activities or support functional units. Because these types of innovation are usually aimed at cost savings and enhancing efficiency, they are often referred to as cost-saving innovations. That being said, the presentation of innovations implemented in support functional units are measured and reported in the context of cost-saving.

Innovation Degree

The preceding section looked at the aspect of *where* innovation occurs or the context in which innovation occurs (i.e., types of innovation). This section looks at *how* innovation occurs in any form or type of innovation. How innovation occurs is referred to as *innovation degree*, and as stated earlier, innovation degree is one of the two concepts of the dimensionality of innovation.

The common categories of the extent of the newness of innovations or innovative ideas are *radical* and *incremental.* These are described as follows:

- *Radical innovation:* This is the highest extent or range of the perceived newness or novelty of an innovative idea in any type of innovation. One of the characteristics of radical innovations is that once launched on the market or implemented in the organization they completely or totally replacing an existing product, service, process, marketing strategy, or customer service element and result in a whole new way of providing a solution to a problem.
- *Incremental innovation:* Generally, this is defined as the extent of the newness or novelty of an innovative idea in which innovative changes or improvements are created or implemented in the existing functional activities of an organization, such as products, services, processes, marketing strategy, and customer service, as well as cost-saving innovations in back-office functional activities.

As you shall see in Steps Two, Three, and Four, the innovation performance measurement model adopted for this book takes into account the innovation degree. Chapter Nine of the *Leadership for Innovation* describes in detail the concept of innovation degree.

Innovation-performance

What is innovation-performance measurement? It is a process that involves reviewing and assessing various innovation performance–related activities at the functional-unit and corporate levels of an organization and then determining the extent to which the goals of the various aspects of innovation activities have been achieved.

Importance of Measuring Innovation Performance

Why is it important to measure and report innovation performance? Six reasons:

- First, the information generated is useful for determining the innovation-performance status of an organization in terms of whether the innovation goals, objectives, and targets that were set by various functional units and the organization as a whole have been achieved.
- Second, information generated from the cross-functional innovation performance reporting and communication system is useful for determining, comprehensively, whether the organization's efforts in investing in innovation activities across functional units are yielding results.
- Third, the innovation performance data can be used for making decisions moving forward, regarding the kind of innovation strategies that should be developed and implemented.
- Fourth, the information generated helps in analyzing variances in innovation performance goals and targets. *What does this mean?* In any kind of performance, the positive deviation from set goals and targets indicates better performance. Conversely, negative deviation is generally a matter of concern because it indicates a shortfall in performance. In terms of innovation performance, the information elicited from innovation performance measurement activities helps determine the kind of decisions that should be made arising from variances in innovation performance goals and targets, especially in cases of negative deviations. This section also provides an evaluation tool (referred to as evaluation worksheets) aimed at eliciting information regarding innovation performance deviations.
- Fifth, similar to the preceding point, measuring innovation helps in determining the kind of corrective actions that should be undertaken, because once the deviations in innovation performance goals and targets are identified, the next step is developing plans for taking corrective

actions. And if the innovation performance is consistently less than what is desired, then a detailed analysis of the factors responsible for such performance must be undertaken.

- Sixth, information collected from measuring innovation performance helps in determining how the company's innovation performance measures up against competitors, and such information is vital for the organization's innovation strategy development.

Structure of the Book

This book is structured in two parts. Part I covers the four metrics of measuring innovation performance arranged in four steps, as follows:

- Step One: Innovation Input Measurement
- Step Two: Innovation Output Measurement
- Step Three: Innovation-Results Measurement
- Step Four: Innovation Impact Measurement

Part II covers some of the vital aspects to consider when structuring an innovation performance report. Please note that for presentational purposes of this book, the contents of Part II appear at the end of the book. When writing the actual innovation performance report, Part II should be used as introduction.

Step One

INNOVATION INPUT MEASUREMENT

Overview

The US publication *strategy+business*, published by Strategy& (formerly Booz & Company), has conducted an annual study on the importance of innovation inputs for more than ten years. Over the years, the studies have consistently revealed that innovation success depends on the company's investments in various innovation-related interventions or inputs. Given how vital innovation inputs are to creating a climate for innovation and sustaining innovation-led growth in organizations, it's important that organizational leaders understand various types of innovation inputs and know how to create a presentation format for reporting innovation input metrics in the context of the organization's value chain and business model. Step One covers (1) definitions of innovation input measurement (2) illustration: how to report innovation input measurements, and (3) innovation input evaluation.

Definitions

To understand innovation input measurement, it is first necessary to define the terms *innovation inputs* and *innovation inputs measurement.*

Definition of *Innovation Inputs*

The basic meaning of the word *inputs*, according to dictionary definitions, varies depending on the context in which the word is being used. According to a number of dictionaries, the term *inputs* means "something that is put in," "to put in," or "an act or process of putting in," with the view of expecting an outcome. Translated in the context of innovation, *innovation inputs* can be defined as various innovation-support systems—such as innovation-related strategies, innovation-related policies and procedures, innovation-enhancing technologies, innovation-skill-development programs, and so forth—that the leadership of an organization implements or invests in across the organization to create a climate for workforce innovation to realize innovation-led growth on an ongoing basis.

Definition of *Innovation Input Measurement*

Therefore, *innovation input measurement* is defined as a process that involves determining and measuring innovation-support systems, such as innovation-support strategies, innovation-support policies and procedures, innovation-skill-development programs, innovation-enhancing technologies, and many other initiatives implemented across functional units during the period under review.

Illustration:
How to Report Innovation Input Measurements

This section illustrates how to determine and report innovation input measurements by presenting innovation-support initiatives implemented over a particular period in the core and support functional units of the fictitious company DM Personal Care Products. To demonstrate this, two types of sample worksheets are provided, as follows:

- Tables 1-1 and 1-2 present the innovation-support initiatives implemented by core and support functional units, respectively, across the organization during the period under review.

- Table 1-3 is the innovation input evaluation worksheet, whose purpose is to assess how the various innovation-support initiatives presented in tables 1-1 and 1-2 were implemented and also to determine the extent to which the intended consequences of the initiatives implemented during the period under review were realized.

The tables have been applied to the functional units of DM Personal Care Products, which are as follows:

Core functional units

- Product-development department
- Manufacturing-processes department
- Marketing department
- Customer service department

Support functional units

- Procurement department
- HR department
- Finance and accounting department
- IT department
- Corporate affairs department

Innovation Inputs Templates

For illustration purposes, three tables are provided, I.e. Tables 1-1, 1-2, and 1-3. The worksheets are segmented into three categories of innovation-support initiatives, and two columns in each worksheet are used to indicate the innovation-support initiatives implemented in the context of each of the three categories—namely innovative thinking–related initiatives, innovation engagement–related initiatives, and innovation management–related initiatives—and the purpose of each innovation-support initiative.

Table 1-1. Innovative Thinking-Related Programs Implemented

Objective: *To determine innovative thinking initiatives implemented in core functional units during the period under review*		
Period under review: *(e.g., February–May of 2021)*		
List of innovative thinking programs implemented	**Name of functional unit** (if the initiative was implemented across the organization, you state-crosscutting)	**State the purpose of each innovation-support initiative**
Questioning attribute	Crosscutting	To implement a range of programs and initiatives aimed at helping workforces develop questioning attributes
The following innovative thinking initiatives would be outlined in a similar way. • Associating attribute • Experimenting attribute • Networking attribute • Envisioning attribute • No fear-for-failure attribute • Risk-taking attribute • Challenging-status-quo attribute • Grit attribute • Thinking time attribute • Educating managers about the importance of role-modelling in leading a culture of innovation		

Table 1-2. Innovation Engagement-Related Programs Implemented

Objective: *To determine innovation engagement initiatives implemented across functional units of the company during the period under review.*		
Period under review: *(e.g., February–May of 2021)*		
Part I **Informative style** Programs aimed at educating and informing workforces about the company`s innovation strategies, practices, policies and procedures		
List of innovation engagement programs implemented	**Name of functional unit** (if the initiative was implemented across the organization, you state-crosscutting)	**State the purpose of each innovation-support initiative**
Publicize and educate workforces about the following innovation management programs implemented by the company: • Innovation priority areas • Interpreting and creating dimensions of innovation • Translating the meaning of innovation • Formulating organizational innovation goals • Creating innovation roles • Creating innovation-challenge questions • Innovation-idea management system • Identifying and hiring innovation talent • Measuring and reporting innovation performance	Crosscutting	To publicize and educate workforces about a range of innovation management programs implemented by the company

table continues on next page

<table>
<tr><td colspan="3">Part II
Inspirational style
The use of innovation-motivating slogans, catchphrases, and visual illustrations to educate and inspire workforces about various aspects of innovation</td></tr>
<tr><th>List of innovation engagement programs implemented</th><th>Name of functional unit
(if the initiative was implemented across the organization, you state -crosscutting)</th><th>State the purpose of each innovation-support initiative</th></tr>
<tr><td>Educate and inspire workforces about the:
• Meaning of innovation in the contexts of the organization`s different functional activities<br>• Dimensions of innovation in the context of the organization`s functional activities
• Significance of innovation
• Link between innovation and realizing organizational vision
• Potential that workforces possess to generate innovative ideas
• The relationship between innovation and organizational growth
• Link between innovation and career growth of workforces</td><td>Crosscutting</td><td>To educate workforces by use of innovation-motivating slogans, catchphrases, and visual illustrations to educate workforces about various aspects of innovation listed in this table</td></tr>
</table>

Table 1-3. Innovation Management-Related Programs Implemented

<table>
<tr><td colspan="3">Objective: To determine innovation management-related initiatives implemented across functional units during the period under review</td></tr>
<tr><td colspan="3">Period under review: (e.g., February–May of 2021)</td></tr>
<tr><th>List of innovation engagement programs implemented</th><th>Name of functional unit
(if the initiative was implemented across the organization, you state -crosscutting)</th><th>State the purpose of each innovation-support initiative</th></tr>
<tr><td>Identified and created innovation priority areas (IPAs) across functional units of the company
• Interpreting and creating dimensions of innovation
• Translating the meaning of innovation in the context of
• Formulating organizational innovation goals
• Creating innovation roles
• Creating innovation-challenge questions
• Innovation-idea management system
• Creating a mechanism for identifying and hiring innovation talent
• Creating a framework for innovation talent succession planning
• Adopting or implementing technology for advancing innovation in the company
• Creating a framework for measuring and reporting innovation performance</td><td>Crosscutting</td><td>To identify areas of high priority for innovation across the organization.</td></tr>
</table>

Evaluation

Before we look at each of the four metrics of innovation-performance measurement, it is necessary to give a brief description of one of the useful tools aligned with the innovation-performance measurement model adopted in this book, the *evaluation worksheet.* As stated in the Introduction of this book, the innovation-performance measurement model suggested in this book is aimed at providing tools for determining the innovation performance of an organization in a multidimensional manner. To enhance the effectiveness of the model, an evaluation worksheet is included for each of the four metrics of innovation-performance measurement. When formulating the actual innovation performance report you may not need to include.

Purpose of the Evaluation Worksheets

It is important to bear in mind that the measurement of innovation performance is not an end in itself. The measurement process merely provides data for determining whether an innovation activity resulted in accomplishing a particular purpose or achieving particular goals. Thus, the worksheets are used to evaluate the data collected through the measurement process.

Contexts of the Evaluation Worksheets

As noted, evaluation worksheets or tables can be used for eliciting and deciphering data generated in each of the four dimensions of innovation-performance measurement. Thus, an evaluation worksheet is included for each of the four dimensions. The evaluation worksheet is formulated and phrased in the context of the innovation measurement under consideration. In other words, each evaluation worksheet is designed to fulfill a distinct objective in relation to the particular dimension of innovation-performance measurement, which is to assess the extent to which the goals and targets for each innovation-performance dimension under consideration were realized or achieved over a particular period.

The evaluation worksheets are contextualized in the four dimensions of innovation-performance measurements as follows:

- *Innovation Input Evaluation Worksheet:* This is designed to assess how various innovation-support initiatives were implemented and also to determine the extent to which the intended consequences of the initiatives were realized during the period under review.
- *Innovation Output Evaluation Worksheet*: This is designed to assess the degree to which innovation output goals and targets were realized.
- *Innovation-Results Evaluation Worksheet:* This is designed to assess the degree to which the innovations launched or implemented (innovation goals or targets) were realized.
- *Innovation Impact Evaluation Worksheet:* This is designed to determine the revenues generated from innovations launched and the savings gained from cost-saving innovations implemented across the functional units of the organization.

Checkpoints

To ensure that each of the evaluation worksheets fulfills its purpose, the following checkpoints should be included in the evaluation worksheets:

- Determining whether the innovation-support initiatives in various functional units were well implemented during the period under review
- Determining the effectiveness of the innovation-support initiatives in terms of realizing the intended consequences
- Determining whether the innovation-support initiatives resulted in unintended consequences
- Identifying gaps and deviations in the innovation-support initiatives implemented in various functional units and determining corrective measures if necessary
- Determining whether the targeted number of radical and incremental innovation ideas generated was achieved and providing an explanation for achieving or missing the target

- Determining whether the targeted number of radical and incremental innovation ideas undergoing development was achieved and providing an explanation for achieving or missing the target
- Determining whether the targeted number of radical and incremental innovations launched or implemented was achieved and providing an explanation for achieving or missing the target
- Determining whether the targeted revenue from innovations launched or the targeted savings from cost-saving innovations implemented across functional units was achieved and providing an explanation for achieving or missing the targets.

We begin with the innovation input evaluation.

Innovation Input Evaluation

As stated earlier, the purpose of the innovation input evaluation is to identify the types of innovation-support initiatives undertaken during the period under review and also to determine the extent to which the intended consequences (the objectives) of the initiatives were realized.

Assuming we are undertaking innovation input evaluation for the core and support (back-office) functional units of DM Personal Care Products, the first step is to outline the core and support functional units, as follows:

Core functional units

- Product-development unit
- Manufacturing-processes department
- Marketing department
- Customer service department

Support functional units

- Procurement department
- HR department

- Finance and accounting department
- IT department
- Corporate affairs department

The second step is creating simple innovation input evaluation worksheets that are categorized according to the types of innovation-support initiatives undertaken. For this illustration, there are three innovation input evaluation worksheets, as follows:

- Table 1-4: Innovative thinking initiatives
- Table 1-5: Innovation engagement initiatives
- Table 1-6: Innovation management initiatives

Table 1-4. Innovative Thinking Initiatives

Name of department: Product development **Segment or unit:**				
State the *innovative thinking initiatives* that were implemented during the period under review (*example initiatives are given here*)	**Implementation:** State whether the initiative was well implemented and whether the initiative has been well adopted in the organization's systems	**Objectives:** State the objectives of the innovation-support initiatives undertaken during the period under review	**Outcomes:** State the extent to which each initiative has contributed to advancing innovation performance in the organization (i.e., the extent to which the initiative has realized the intended purpose)	**Improvements:** State aspects of the initiative that need to be improved if the program is to be effective
Questioning skills program				
Observing skills program				
Associating skills program				
Discovering skills program				
Envisioning skills program				
Experimenting skills program				
Networking skills program				
Head of department: Date:				

Table 1-5. Innovation Engagement Initiatives

Name of department: Product development **Segment or unit:**				
State the *innovation engagement initiatives* that were implemented during the period under review (*example initiatives are given here*)	**Implementation:** State whether the initiative was well implemented and whether the initiative has been well adopted in the organization's systems	**Objectives:** State the objectives of the innovation-support initiatives undertaken during the period under review	**Outcomes:** State the extent to which each initiative has contributed to advancing innovation performance in the organization (i.e., the extent to which the initiative has realized the intended purpose)	**Improvements:** State aspects of the initiative that need to be improved if the program is to be effective
Program for educating workforces on the meaning of *innovation*				
Program for promoting the significance of innovation				
Program for educating workforces on types of innovation				

table continues on next page

State the *innovation engagement initiatives* that were implemented during the period under review (*example initiatives are given here*)	**Implementation:** State whether the initiative was well implemented and whether the initiative has been well adopted in the organization's systems	**Objectives:** State the objectives of the innovation-support initiatives undertaken during the period under review	**Outcomes:** State the extent to which each initiative has contributed to advancing innovation performance in the organization (i.e., the extent to which the initiative has realized the intended purpose)	**Improvements:** State aspects of the initiative that need to be improved if the program is to be effective
Program for educating workforces on innovation degree				
Program for promoting the connection between vision and innovation				
Head of department: Date:				

Table 1-6. Innovation Management Initiatives

Name of department: Product development **Segment or unit:**				
State the *innovation management initiatives* that were implemented during the period under review (*example initiatives are given here*)	**Implementation:** State whether the initiative was well implemented and whether the initiative has been well adopted in the organization's systems	**Objectives:** State the objectives of the innovation-support initiatives undertaken during the period under review	**Outcomes:** State the extent to which the initiative has contributed to advancing innovation performance in the organization (i.e., the extent to which the initiative has realized the intended purpose)	**Improvements:** State aspects of the initiative that need to be improved if the program is to be more effective
Visually illustrated chart showing functional-unit priority areas on which to focus innovation				
Innovation-performance job descriptions and job specifications in job positions across functional units				

table continues on next page

State the *innovation management initiatives* that were implemented during the period under review (*example initiatives are given here*)	**Implementation:** State whether the initiative was well implemented and whether the initiative has been well adopted in the organization's systems	**Objectives:** State the objectives of the innovation-support initiatives undertaken during the period under review	**Outcomes:** State the extent to which the initiative has contributed to advancing innovation performance in the organization (i.e., the extent to which the initiative has realized the intended purpose)	**Improvements:** State aspects of the initiative that need to be improved if the program is to be more effective
Innovation-challenge-questions system across functional units				
Framework for formulating corporate and functional-unit innovation goals				
Innovation-idea-management system				
Workforce-diversity framework for advancing innovation across functional units				

table continues on next page

State the *innovation management initiatives* that were implemented during the period under review (*example initiatives are given here*)	**Implementation:** State whether the initiative was well implemented and whether the initiative has been well adopted in the organization's systems	**Objectives:** State the objectives of the innovation-support initiatives undertaken during the period under review	**Outcomes:** State the extent to which the initiative has contributed to advancing innovation performance in the organization (i.e., the extent to which the initiative has realized the intended purpose)	**Improvements:** State aspects of the initiative that need to be improved if the program is to be more effective
Framework for identifying and determining innovation talent in job candidates				
Framework for evaluating innovation performance of workforces				
Innovation-talent-succession planning framework				
Functional-unit innovation strategies				

table continues on next page

State the *innovation management initiatives* that were implemented during the period under review (*example initiatives are given here*)	**Implementation:** State whether the initiative was well implemented and whether the initiative has been well adopted in the organization's systems	**Objectives:** State the objectives of the innovation-support initiatives undertaken during the period under review	**Outcomes:** State the extent to which the initiative has contributed to advancing innovation performance in the organization (i.e., the extent to which the initiative has realized the intended purpose)	**Improvements:** State aspects of the initiative that need to be improved if the program is to be more effective
Framework for measuring and reporting innovation performance across functional units				
Head of department: Date:				

Step Two

INNOVATION OUTPUT MEASUREMENT

Overview

The basic meaning of the word *output*, according to dictionary definitions, varies depending on the context in which the word is being used. According to the *Merriam-Webster* online dictionary, the generic definition of *output* is "the amount of something that is produced depending on the context of what it is."

Contexts of outputs range from basic things like outputs of corn, rice, oranges, and tomatoes in an agricultural context to outputs of gold, copper, and diamonds in a mineral context to the more complex contexts, such as the work output of a machine in engineering terms or the transmission of information in an IT context. In economic terms, output is the amount of goods and services produced, whereas in a telecommunications context, output entails information retrieved from a network. The point is that the term *output* is context specific, and the list of contexts of outputs goes on and on. So, Step Two covers (1) definitions of the terms innovation output and innovation output measurement (2) two perspectives of innovation output: number of innovation ideas generated and number of innovation ideas undergoing development (3) illustration: how to present radical and incremental innovation ideas (4) How to present number of innovation ideas undergoing development (5) determining radical and incremental innovation ideas undergoing development in support functional units (6) innovation output evaluation worksheet.

Definitions

To understand innovation output measurement, it is first necessary to define the terms *innovation output* and *innovation output measurement.*

Definition of *Innovation Output*

In the context of measuring innovation, *innovation output* is defined as the number of innovation ideas generated in the context of the organization's value chain and business segments.

The preceding section noted that innovation input measurement involves assessing various innovation-support initiatives undertaken over a specific period. Therefore, the first evidence to manifest as a consequence of the innovation inputs is the generation of innovation ideas by workforces—hence the characterization of innovation ideas generated as innovation outputs, because they're a result of the specific innovation initiatives undertaken.

Definition of *Innovation Output Measurement*

Given the context of innovation outputs, *innovation output measurement* can be defined as a process that involves determining the number of innovation ideas generated by workforces across functional units as a consequence of the various innovation-support initiatives implemented by the organization over a particular period.

Two Perspectives of Innovation Output

In this book, innovation output is divided into two perspectives: (1) the number of innovation ideas *generated* by workforces over a particular period, and (2) the number of innovation ideas *undergoing development.*

1. Number of Innovation Ideas Generated

It's important to understand that determining the number of innovation ideas generated is one of the vital aspects of measuring and reporting innovation performance. This is because if the information on innovation ideas generated is poorly determined and presented, it could potentially negatively affect the quality and accuracy of the data about the number of innovation ideas generated and consequently affect the quality of the innovation-performance report. To avoid this, the teams directly responsible for compiling the organization's innovation-performance report need to do it competently by enacting measures that will contribute to ensuring the quality and accuracy of the data collected on the innovation ideas generated across functional units. Some considerations include the following:

- *Cross-functional collaboration:* This entails building and sustaining the process and spirit of working together with functional leaders when collecting data on innovation ideas generated across functional units. The earlier discussion of innovation-idea management systems suggested an elaborate approach for establishing various innovation-idea management committees as part of the corporate strategy for sustaining an effective innovation-idea management system. It was further stated that collaboration among functional units is vital in ensuring that an organization has an effective innovation-idea management system. In relation to collecting data on the number of innovation ideas generated over a particular period, it is important that those responsible for writing innovation-performance reports (especially at the corporate level) must ensure that they collaborate with all stakeholders involved—that is, functional units and various innovation-related committees—to, for instance, ascertain the number of ideas generated in each functional unit over a particular period.
- *Designing the right presentation format:* This means ensuring that the right type of format or technique is used to present the number of innovation ideas generated across functional units. Generally, one of the purposes of reporting innovation performance in organizations is to

enable every member of the organization's workforce, from CEO to the most junior, to understand all aspects of the organization's innovation performance. Data presentation therefore plays a critical role in realizing the purpose of reporting innovation performance in the organization. Thus, the data-presentation format or techniques must ensure that data are presented in a simple, creative, and interesting manner, without the audiences across functional units having to work hard to understand the data presented about the number of innovation ideas and other dimensions of innovation-performance measurements.

Illustration:
How to Present Radical and Incremental Innovation Ideas

This section demonstrates how to determine and present the number of radical and incremental innovation ideas generated across functional units in the context of the four core functional units and five support functional units of DM Personal Care Products. The steps in the process are presented first.

Steps

- First, identify core and support functional units of the company.
- Second, structure the presentation format according to the functional units of the company.
- Third, outline the company's product platforms.

Recall that the core and support functional units of DM Personal Care Products are as follows:

Core functional units

- Product-development unit, with the following segments:
    - Body-lotions segment
    - Skin-cleansing segment
    - Hair-care segment
    - Hand-washing segment

- Manufacturing-processes department, (the manufacturing-processes department comprises the same segments as the product-development unit)
- Marketing department, with the following units:
    - Pricing unit
    - Product-promotion unit
    - New-markets unit
    - Product-delivery unit
    - Packaging unit
- Customer service department

Support functional units

- Procurement department
- HR department
- Finance and accounting department
- IT department
- Corporate affairs department

Presentation Format

Regarding presentation format, assume that simple charts have been selected for use in presenting the number of radical and incremental innovation ideas generated over a particular period in each of the core and support functional units of DM Personal Care Products. We'll begin with core functional units and then move to the support units. Specifically, we'll start with the product-development unit.

Product-Development Unit

The first step is to determine the number of product categories and segments in the product-development unit. The following are the product categories of the department under consideration:

- Body-lotions category
- Skin-cleansing category

- Hair-care category
- Hand-washing category

The second step is to create simple charts for presenting the number of radical and incremental product innovation ideas generated in each of these product categories during the period under review. For purposes of illustration, we'll assume quarterly review in four segments: Q1, Q2, Q3, and Q4. For illustration purposes, innovation ideas in the body-lotions category are referred to as *radical* and *incremental body-lotion innovation ideas*.

The two simple charts in figures 2-1 and 2-2 show radical and incremental body-lotion innovation ideas generated in the body-lotions category in each quarter of 2021. The charts show both the target and actual numbers of innovation ideas generated.

Figure 2-1

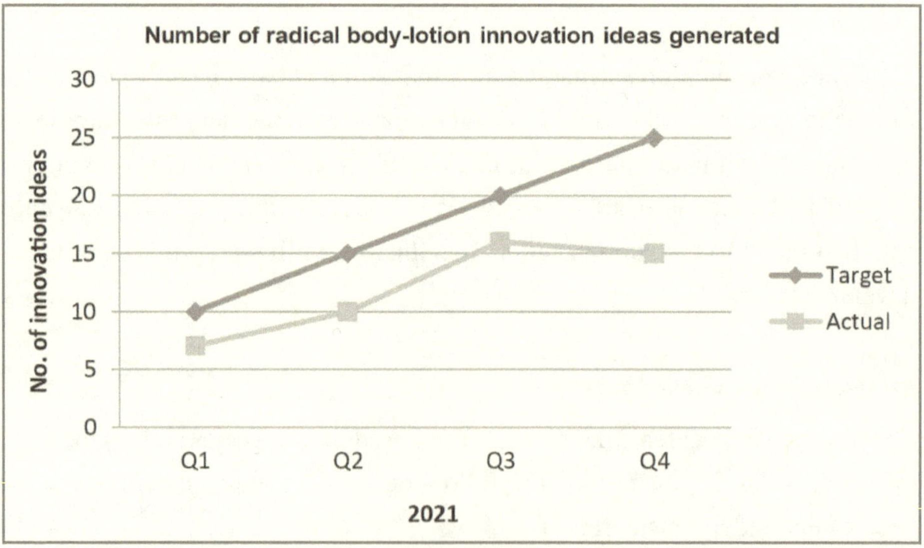

Number of radical body-lotion innovation ideas generated

No. of innovation ideas
30
25
20
15
10
5
0
Q1
Q2
Q3
Q4
2021
Target
Actual

Figure 2-2

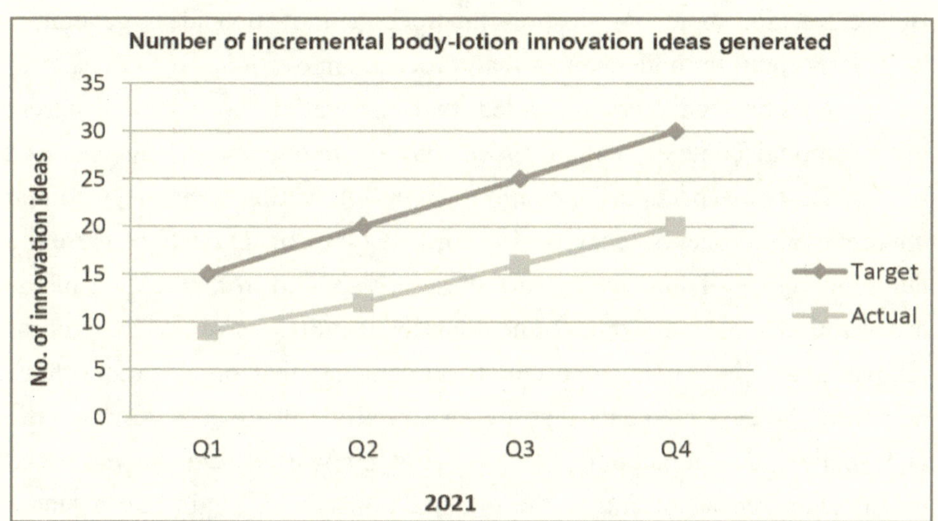

Similar charts would be created to show the number of radical and incremental innovation ideas generated in each of the other three product categories over the same period:

- Skin-cleansing category
- Hair-care category
- Hand-washing category

There are cases where a product category may have a number of product segments. In such cases, the number of radical and incremental innovation ideas generated should be determined per product segment of the particular product category. For instance, under its new corporate structure (with Alphabet as parent company), Google has six product categories: Android, Search, YouTube, Apps, Maps, and Ads. Each of these categories has product segments, and if we were to determine the number of innovation ideas generated, we would determine the number of innovation ideas generated in all product segments of each product category.

Manufacturing-Processes Department

Before we talk about how to present process innovation ideas generated, it is important to understand what process innovations are. Recall, in the introduction chapter we stated that innovation occurs in different organizational contexts, called *dimensions of innovation*. A concept used to describe two aspects of innovation: *where* innovation occurs (types) *and how* innovation occurs (degree). In terms of types of innovation, there are numerous types of innovation, and these are applied in the context of the organization`s business model and functional units. So, what are process innovations? First, it is important to understand that organizations have numerous process elements that are structurally embedded across its core and support functional units, and process innovations can be described or characterized according to the organization's value chain and business model. Second, process activities vary from company to company depending on the type and nature of an organization. For instance, the core and support process activities of a telecom company like AT&T will differ from those of a company in the auto industry like GM. Similarly, the core and support process activities of a financial-sector company like Bank of America will differ from those of a technology company like Apple. Third, process activities are usually out of view of customers, and in most cases, they influence the delivery of services or products in varying ways depending on the value chain and business model of the organization.

The bottom line is that ideas for process innovations generated in core and support functional activities vary from company to company depending on the type and nature of an organization. A manufacturing company like DM Personal Care Products has manufacturing processes in the context of the company`s business model. DM Personal Care Products has four main manufacturing-processes categories in line with the four product categories in the product-development department:

- Body-lotions manufacturing-processes category
- Skin-cleansing manufacturing-processes category

- Hair-care manufacturing-processes category
- Hand-washing manufacturing-processes category

As with the product-development unit, two simple charts can be used to illustrate the number of radical and incremental innovation ideas generated in these four manufacturing-processes categories in each quarter of 2021. For illustration purposes, figures 2-3 and 2-4 show the radical and incremental innovation ideas generated in the body-lotions manufacturing-processes category in each quarter of 2021.

Figure 2-3

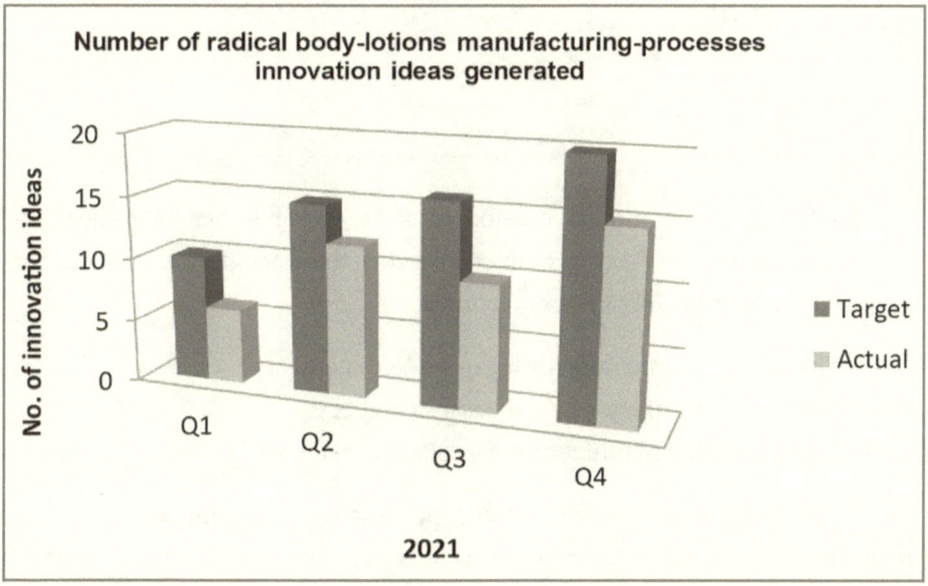

Figure 2-4

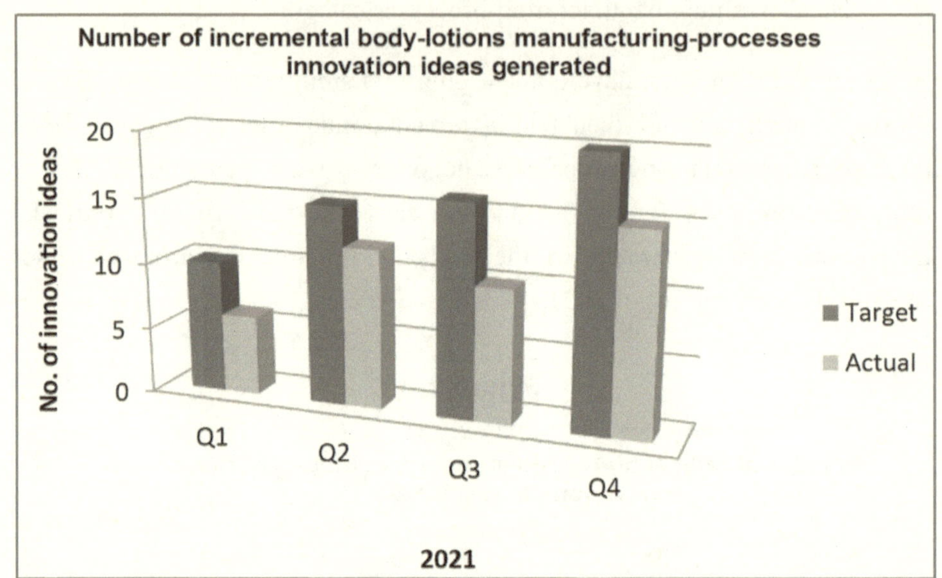

Similar charts would be created to show the number of radical and incremental innovation ideas generated in each of the other three manufacturing-processes categories over the same period:

- Skin-cleansing manufacturing-processes category
- Hair-care manufacturing-processes category
- Hand-washing manufacturing-processes category

As in the first illustration for the product-development unit, there are instances where a manufacturing-processes category may have a number of product-manufacturing segments. In such cases, the number of radical and incremental innovation ideas generated should be determined per the product-manufacturing segment of the particular manufacturing-processes category.

Marketing Department

Recall that this department has five main marketing-related functional subunits, structured as follows:

- Pricing unit
- Product-promotion unit

- Product-delivery unit
- New-markets unit
- Packaging unit

Similar to the presentation format used for the first two functional units, the two simple charts in figures 15-5 and 15-6 present the number of radical and incremental pricing innovation ideas generated for each quarter of 2021.

Figure 2-5

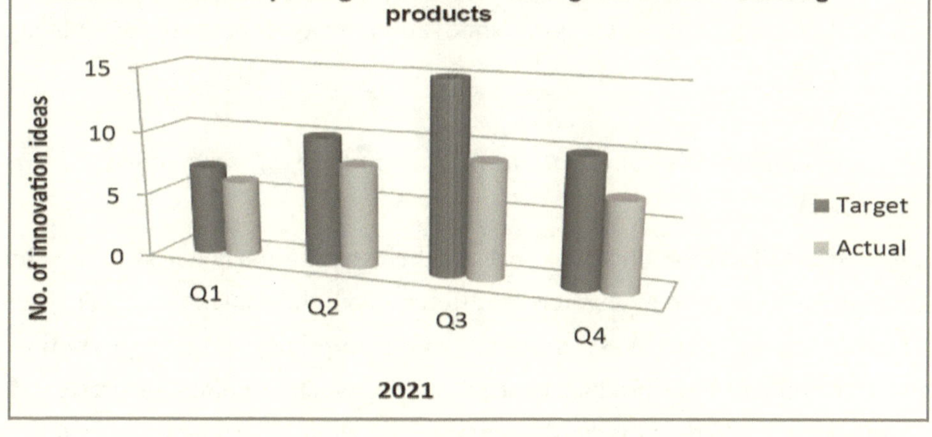

Figure 2-6

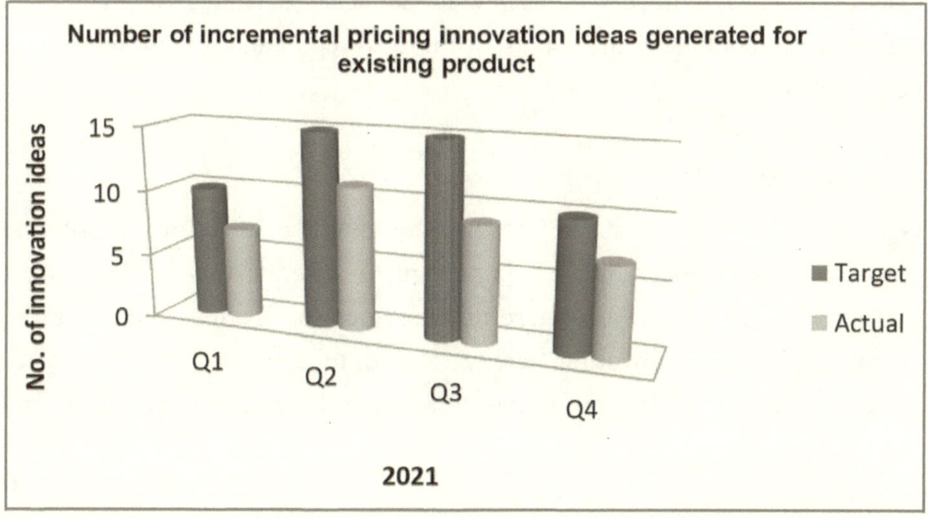

Similar charts would be created to illustrate the number of radical and incremental marketing innovation ideas generated in each of the other four functional subunits of the marketing department in each quarter of 2021. The other marketing functional subunits and the type of innovation ideas (in parentheses) that would be generated in each unit are as follows:

- Product-promotion unit (product-promotion innovation ideas generated for existing products
- Product-delivery unit (product-delivery innovation ideas generated for existing products)
- Packaging unit (packaging innovation ideas generated for existing products)

How to characterize innovation in the context of new market ideas generated

The context of interpreting or expressing the extent of the newness or novelty of an innovation for new markets is different from the contexts of other types of marketing innovations, such as innovations in pricing, product promotion, product delivery, and product packaging. So, when it comes to presenting innovations about new markets discovered for existing products, the phrases *new unserved market* and *new-market segment* are used to characterize the extent of newness or novelty of the new-market ideas generated. Step Three has defined with more detail the contexts of how to report and present innovative new markets.

Customer Service Department

Before we look at how to present the number of customer service innovation ideas generated, it's important to reiterate two of the aspects that were described earlier regarding customer service innovations. First, customer service innovations are designed to support the delivery of product offerings at different stages: before purchase, during purchase, and after purchase. Second is that some customer service innovations (usually referred to as *customer experience innovations*) are implemented across all organizational functions and channels and are designed to continually enhance the quality of interaction between the company and its customers at all touchpoints.

The importance of understanding this is that the customer service innovation ideas generated should be presented according to the customer service components. For illustration purposes, the customer service innovation ideas generated could be presented according to the following categories:

- Customer service innovation ideas designed to support the delivery of product offerings *before* purchase
- Customer service innovation ideas designed to support the delivery of product offerings *during* purchase
- Customer service innovation ideas designed to support the delivery of product offerings *after* purchase
- Customer service innovation ideas aimed at improving the quality of interaction between the company and its customers at all touchpoints

Presentation Format

Let's assume we are determining customer service innovation ideas aimed at supporting the delivery of product offerings before purchase. As in the earlier examples, the before-purchase innovation ideas can be organized into two categories: *before-purchase radical customer service innovation ideas* and *before-purchase incremental customer service innovation ideas*.

Figures 2-7 and 2-8 illustrate the number of radical and incremental customer service innovation ideas generated in each quarter of 2021.

Figure 2-7

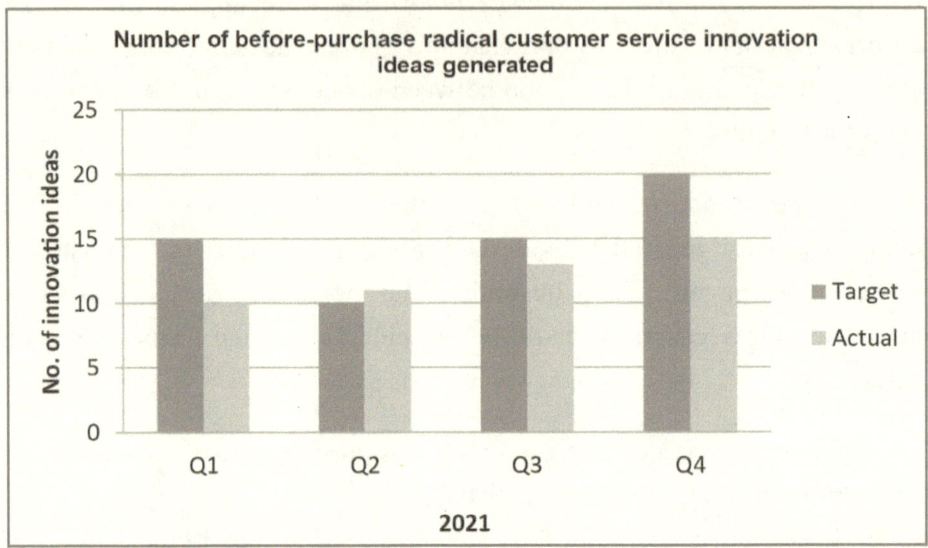

Figure 2-8

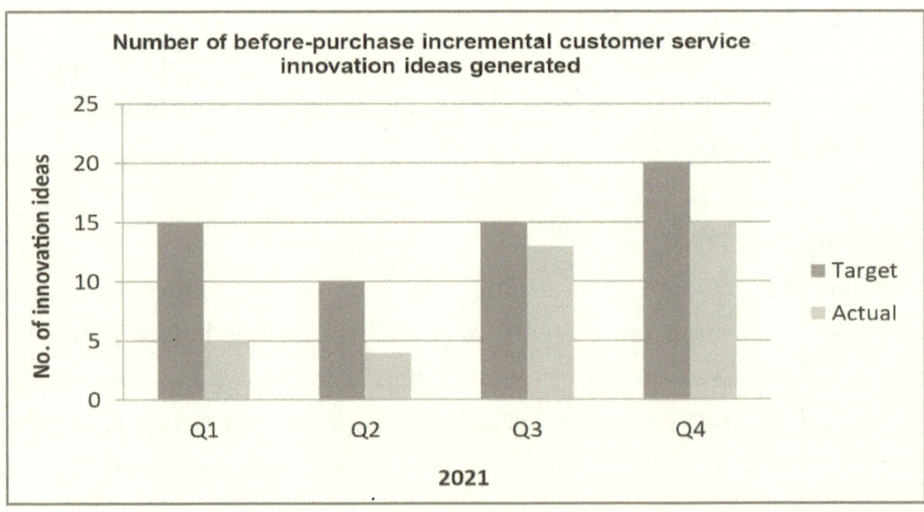

Similar charts would be created to show the number of radical and incremental customer service innovation ideas generated in each of the other three components during the same period:

- Customer service innovation ideas designed to support the delivery of product offerings during purchase
- Customer service innovation ideas designed to support the delivery of product offerings after purchase
- Customer service innovation ideas aimed at improving the quality of interaction between the company and its customers at all touchpoints

Presenting Radical and Incremental Innovation Ideas Generated in Support Functional Units

As mentioned, support functional units play a vital role in implementing innovation-support strategies for creating a climate to advance innovation across functional units. Thus, in addition to implementing innovation-support initiatives, organizational leaders should encourage the generation of cost-saving innovation ideas and other efficiency-related innovation ideas in support functional units.

Therefore, this section shows how to present data on the cost-saving innovation ideas generated in the five support functional units of DM Personal Care Products:

- Procurement department
- HR department
- Finance and accounting department
- IT department
- Corporate affairs department

Figures 2-9 and 2-10 illustrate how to present the number of radical and incremental cost-saving innovation ideas generated in support functional units over a particular period. For illustration purposes, the procurement department is used as an example to show the number of radical and incremental procurement innovation ideas generated in each quarter of 2021.

Figure 2-9

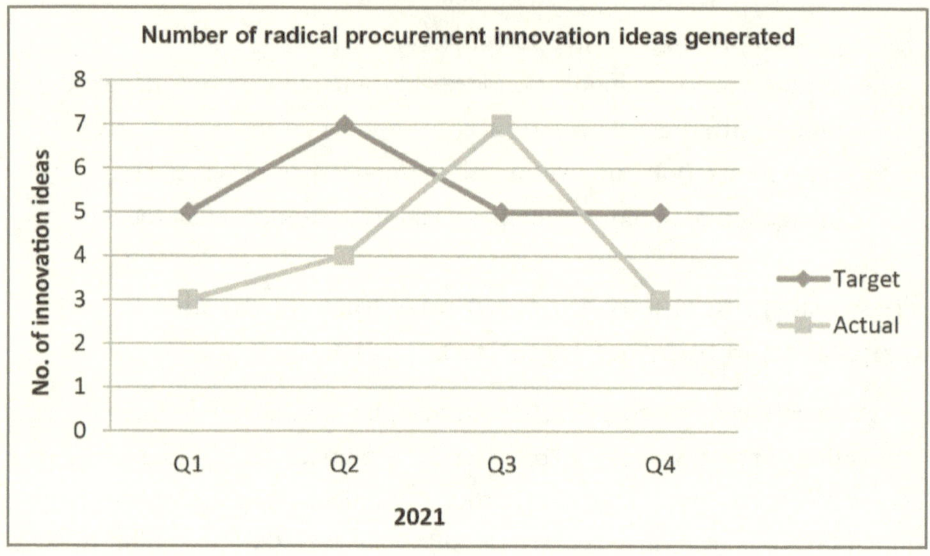

Figure 2-10

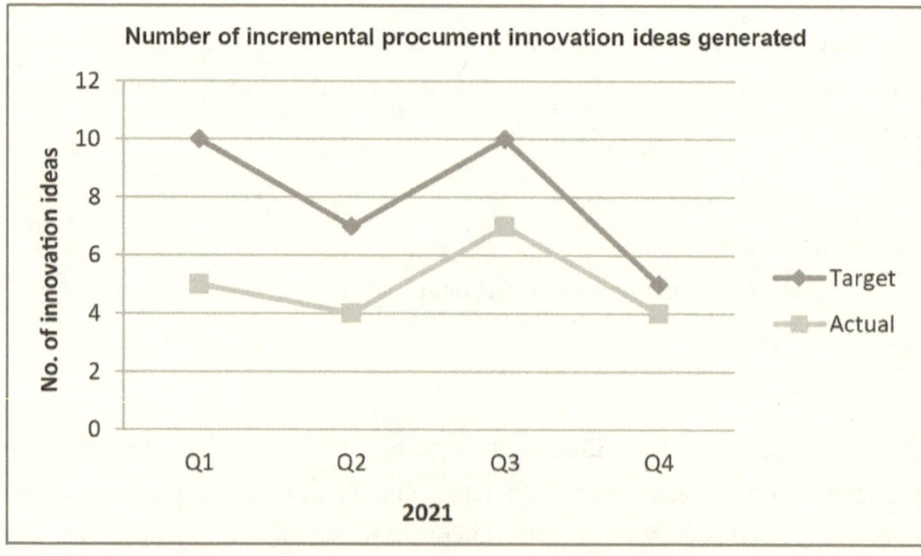

Similar charts would be created to illustrate the number of radical and incremental cost-saving innovation ideas generated in each of the other four support functional units in each quarter of 2021. The other support functional units and the type of innovation ideas (in parentheses) that would be generated for each support unit are as follows:

- HR department (*cost-saving HR innovation ideas*)
- Finance and accounting department (*cost-saving accounting innovation ideas*)
- IT department (*cost-saving IT innovation ideas*)
- Corporate affairs department (*cost-saving corporate affairs innovation ideas*)

2. Number of Innovation Ideas Undergoing Development

Once the information on the number of radical and incremental innovation ideas generated has been presented, the next step is to determine the number, type, and degree of innovation ideas undergoing development during the period under review. Thus, the second context of innovation output measurement involves determining and presenting the number of radical and incremental innovation ideas undergoing development in the innovation-development process over a particular period.

As in previous sections, we'll use the core and support functional units of DM Personal Care Products to illustrate how to present the number of radical and incremental innovation ideas undergoing development. The presentation begins with the core functional units and then covers the support functional units, which are as follows:

Core functional units

- Product-development unit, with the following segments:
  - Body-lotions segment
  - Skin-cleansing segment

  - Hair-care segment
  - Hand-washing segment
- Manufacturing-processes department
- Marketing department, with the following units:
  - Pricing unit
  - Product-promotion unit
  - Product-delivery unit
  - New-markets unit
  - Packaging unit
- Customer service department

Product-Development Department

Similar to the previous examples of determining and presenting the number of ideas generated, the following charts illustrate how to present the number of radical and incremental innovation ideas undergoing development in each of the following product categories of the product-development unit:

- Body-lotions category
- Skin-cleansing category
- Hair-care category
- Hand-washing category

Figures 2-11 and 2-12 illustrate the number of radical and incremental body-lotion innovation ideas undergoing development in each quarter of 2021 (target and actual).

Figure 2-11

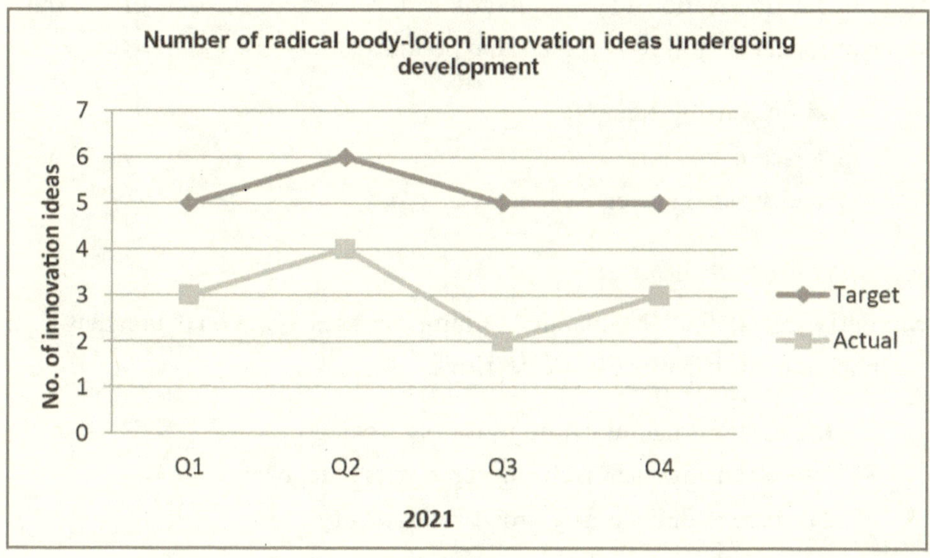

Figure 2-12

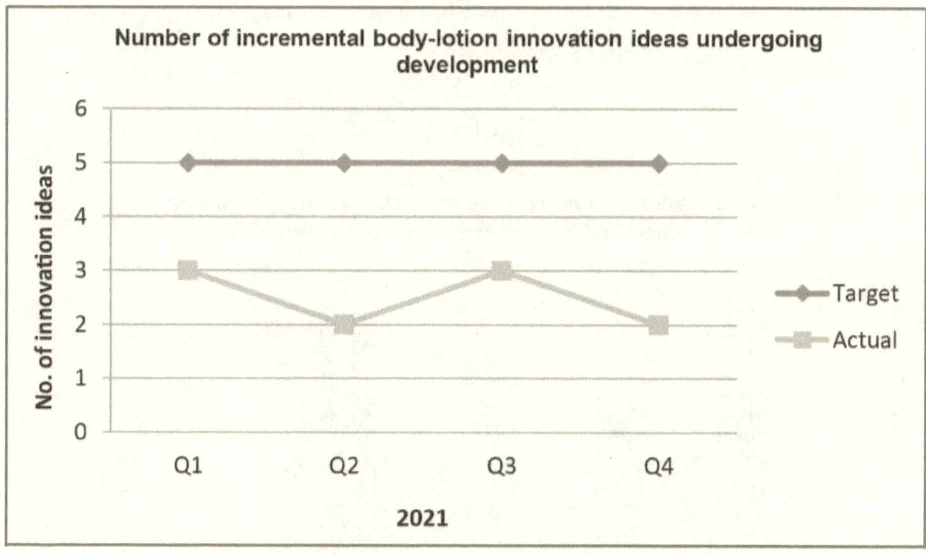

Similar charts would be created to show the number of radical and incremental innovation ideas undergoing development in each of the other three product categories over the same period:

- Skin-cleansing category
- Hair-care category
- Hand-washing category

Manufacturing Department

Similarly, recall that the manufacturing-processes functional unit has four main manufacturing-processes categories:

- Body-lotions manufacturing-processes category
- Skin-cleansing manufacturing-processes category
- Hair-care manufacturing-processes category
- Hand-washing manufacturing-processes category

The simple charts in figures 2-13 and 2-14 illustrate the number of radical and incremental body-lotions innovation ideas undergoing development in each quarter of 2021, (target and actual).

Figure 2-13

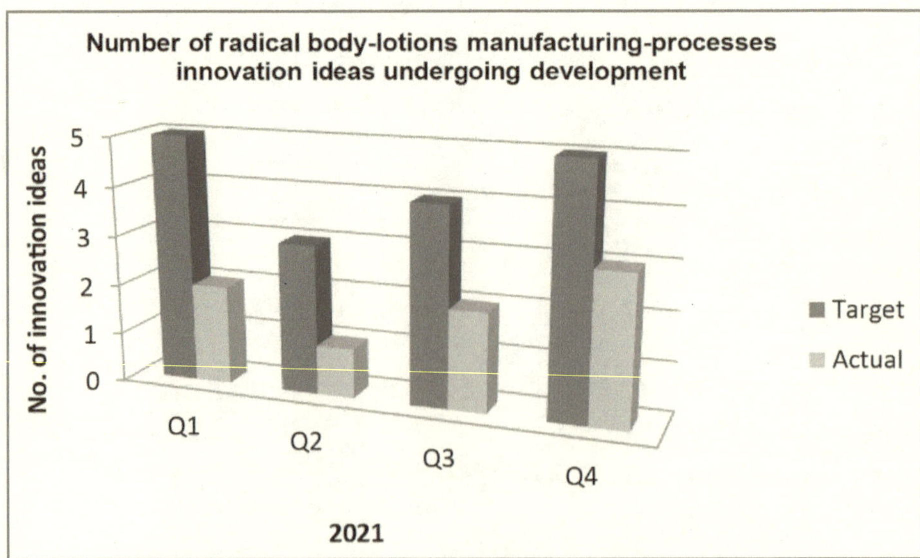

Figure 2-14

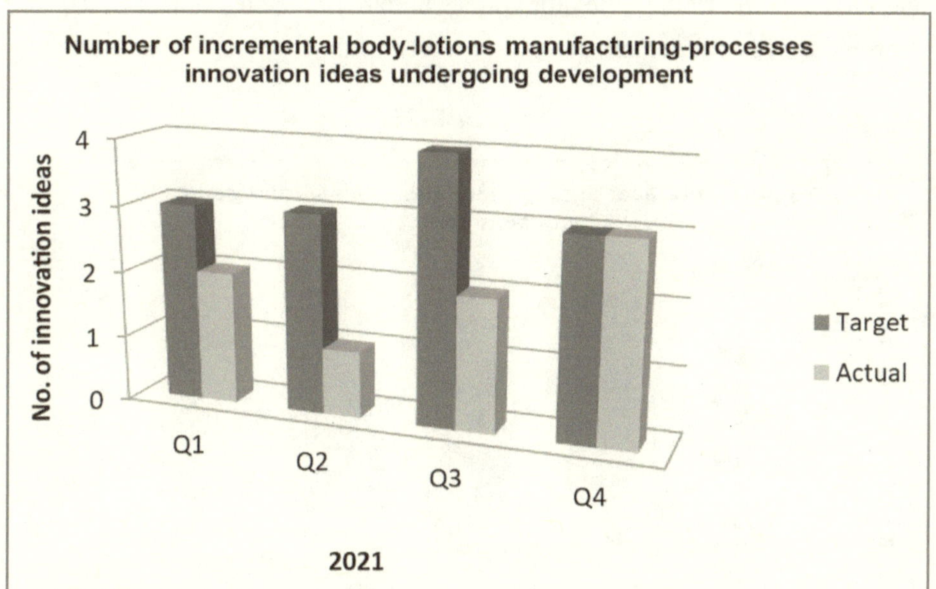

Similar charts would be created to show the number of radical and incremental innovation ideas undergoing development in each of the other three manufacturing-processes categories over the same period:

- Skin-cleansing manufacturing-processes category
- Hair-care manufacturing-processes category
- Hand-washing manufacturing-processes category

Marketing Department

The third example shows how to present the number of radical and incremental marketing innovation ideas undergoing development in each of the five marketing-related functional subunits:

- Pricing unit
- Product-promotion unit
- Product-delivery unit
- New-markets unit
- Packaging unit

The two charts in figures 2-15 and 2-16 present the number of radical and incremental pricing innovation ideas undergoing development in the four quarters of 2021 (target and actual).

Figure 2-15

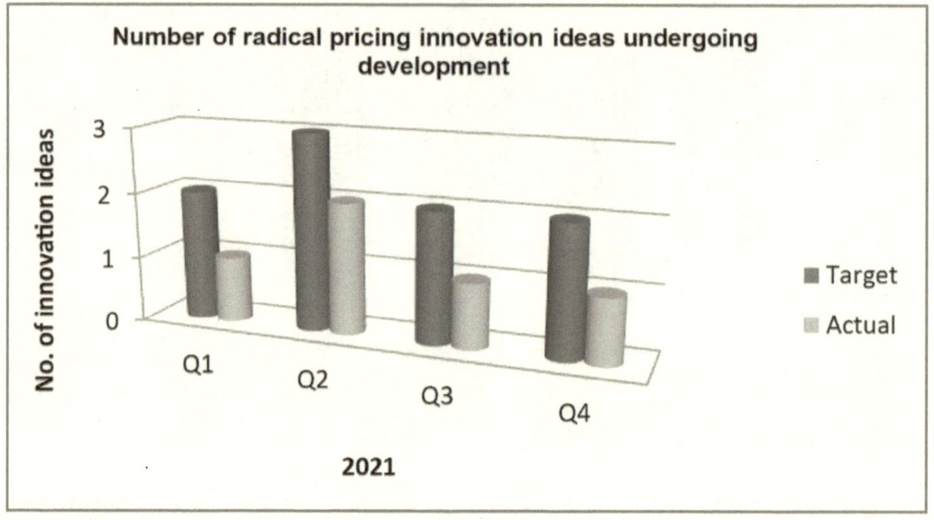

Figure 2-16

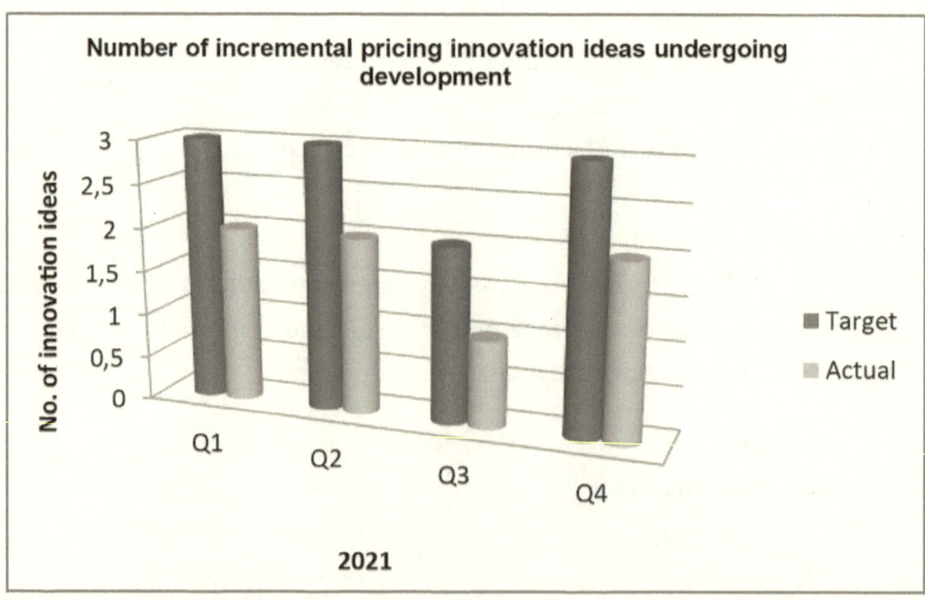

Similar charts would be created to illustrate the number of radical and incremental marketing innovation ideas undergoing development in each of the other four marketing functional subunits:

- Product-promotion unit (product-promotion innovation ideas undergoing development for existing products)
- Product-delivery unit (product-delivery innovation ideas undergoing development for existing products)
- New-markets unit (new-market innovation ideas undergoing development for existing products)
- Packaging unit (packaging innovation ideas undergoing development for existing products)

Customer Service Department

The earlier discussion of the presentation format for innovation ideas generated in the customer service department outlined four aspects to bear in mind when presenting the number of customer service innovation ideas generated. Similarly, when presenting the number of customer service innovation ideas undergoing development, it's important to bear in mind how the customer service segments of an organization are structured. This will enable you to format the presentation of customer service innovation ideas undergoing development according to the customer service segments.

The customer service innovation ideas undergoing development could be categorized as follows:

- Customer service innovation ideas undergoing development designed to support the delivery of product offerings *before purchase*
- Customer service innovation ideas undergoing development designed to support the delivery of product offerings *during purchase*
- Customer service innovation ideas undergoing development designed to support the delivery of product offerings *after purchase*

- Customer service innovation ideas undergoing development aimed at improving the quality of interaction between the company and its customers at all touchpoints

Presentation Format

Let's assume we are determining the number of customer service innovation ideas undergoing development aimed at supporting the delivery of product offerings before purchase.

The two simple charts in figures 2-17 and 2-18 present the number of before-purchase radical and incremental customer service innovation ideas undergoing development in the four quarters of 2021 (target and actual).

Figure 2-17

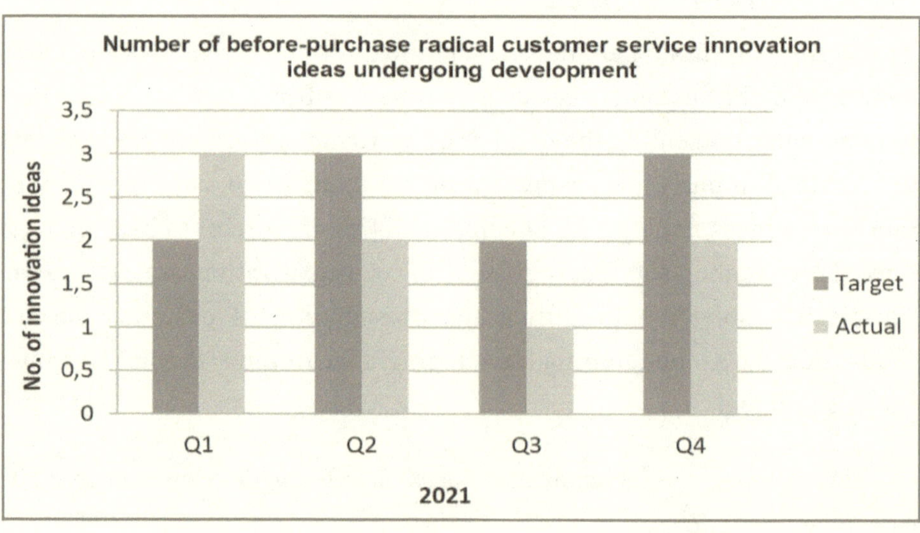

Figure 2-18

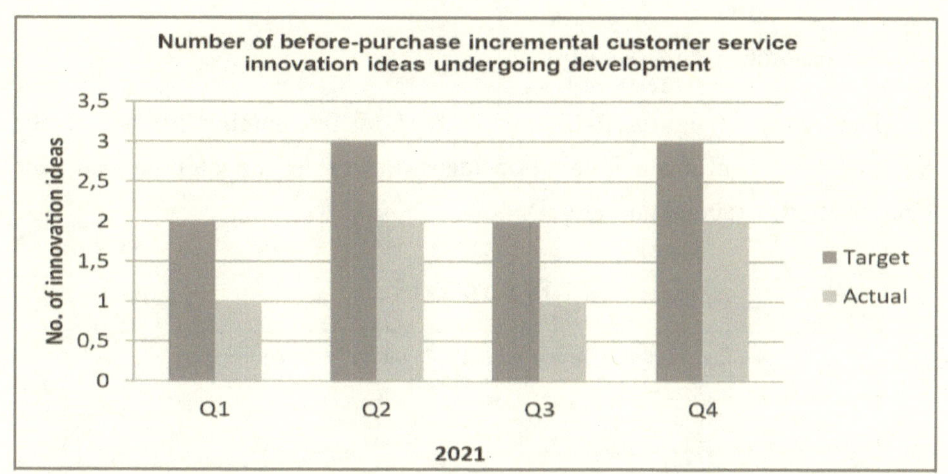

Similar charts would be created for each of the other three customer service categories:

- Customer service innovation ideas undergoing development designed to support the delivery of product offerings during purchase
- Customer service innovation ideas undergoing development designed to support the delivery of product offerings after purchase
- Customer service innovation ideas undergoing development aimed at improving the quality of interaction between the company and its customers at all touchpoints

Determining Radical and Incremental Innovation Ideas Undergoing Development in Support Functional Units

Recall that innovation ideas generated in support functional units are usually focused on cost savings and efficiency. This section looks at how to determine and present cost-saving innovation ideas undergoing development in the support functional units of DM Personal Care Products, which are as follows:

- Procurement department
- HR department

- Finance and accounting department
- IT department
- Corporate affairs department

The charts in figures 2-19 and 2-20 show the number of radical and incremental procurement innovation ideas undergoing development in each quarter of 2021 (actual and target).

Figure 2-19

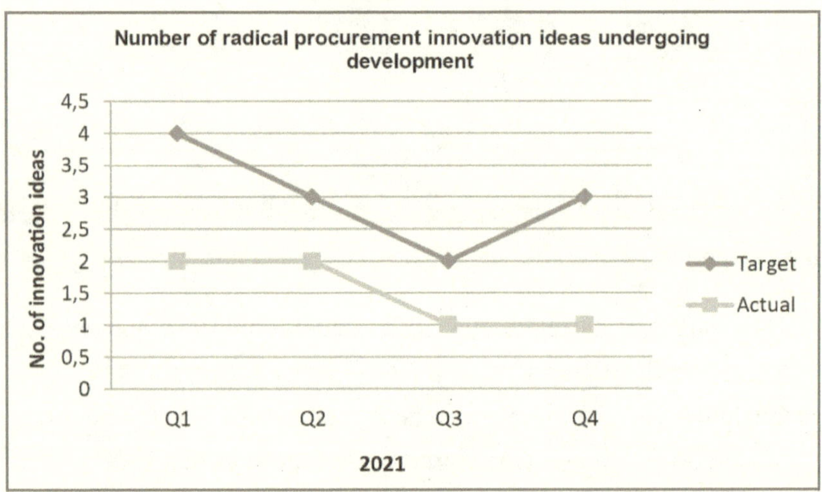

Figure 2-20

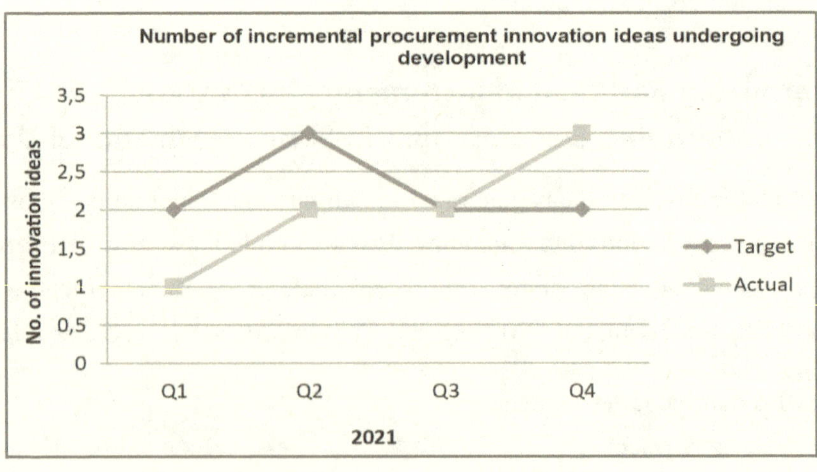

Similar charts would be created for each of the other four support functional units:

- HR department (cost-saving HR innovation ideas)
- Finance and accounting department (cost-saving finance and accounting innovation ideas)
- IT department (cost-saving IT innovation ideas)
- Corporate affairs department (cost-saving corporate affairs innovation ideas)

Innovation Output Evaluation

The beginning of chapter two noted that each of the four metrics of measuring innovation performance has an accompanying evaluation worksheet (e.g., the innovation input evaluation worksheet at the end of the section on innovation input measurement). Thus, once you have determined the number of ideas generated and the number of ideas undergoing development over a particular period, the next activity is to determine whether the *target number of ideas generated* and *target number of ideas undergoing development* over a particular period were achieved. That's where the innovation output evaluation is applied. The example of the innovation output evaluation worksheet in this section is divided into two stand-alone worksheets: an *innovation output evaluation worksheet for ideas generated* and an *innovation output evaluation worksheet for ideas undergoing development.*

Innovation Output Evaluation for Ideas Generated

Tables 2-7 through 2-9 show examples of the innovation output evaluation worksheet for assessing whether the target number of innovation ideas generated was achieved in both the core and support functional units of DM Personal Care Products over a particular period. For illustration purposes, the evaluation worksheet is applied to three of the functional units: the product-development unit (Table 2-7), the marketing department (Table 2-8), and the procurement department (Table 2-9).

Table 2-7. Example of Innovation Output Evaluation for Product Innovation Ideas

<table>
<tr><td colspan="5">Name of Department: Product-development unit

Date: April 30, 2021</td></tr>
<tr><td colspan="5">Purpose of evaluation: To assess whether the target or goal of generating a particular number of radical and incremental product innovation ideas during the period under review (e.g., January–April of 2021) was achieved

The segments of the product-development unit of DM Personal Care Products are presented in the worksheet as follows:
• Part A: Body-lotions segment
• Part B: Skin-cleansing segment
• Part C: Hair-care segment
• Part D: Hand-washing segment</td></tr>
<tr><td colspan="5">Part A

Number of radical and incremental product innovation ideas generated in the body-lotions segment</td></tr>
<tr><td colspan="5">Radical: Number of radical innovation ideas generated during the period under review</td></tr>
<tr><td rowspan="2">Radical innovation ideas generated in the body-lotions segment:

Was the target for this product category achieved? (check "Yes" or "No")</td><td>Yes</td><td>Comment</td><td>No</td><td>Comment</td></tr>
<tr><td></td><td>If yes, indicate the percentage achieved.

Reasons: What factors are responsible for achieving or exceeding the set target?</td><td></td><td>If no, by what percentage was the target missed?

Reasons: What factors are responsible for not meeting the projected target?</td></tr>
</table>

table continues on next page

<table>
<tr><td colspan="5">Incremental: Number of incremental innovation ideas generated during the period under review</td></tr>
<tr><td rowspan="2">Incremental innovation ideas generated in the body-lotions segment:
Was the target for this product category achieved? (check "Yes" or "No")</td><td>Yes</td><td>Comment</td><td>No</td><td>Comment</td></tr>
<tr><td></td><td>If yes, indicate the percentage achieved.
Reasons: What factors are responsible for achieving or exceeding the set target?</td><td></td><td>If no, by what percentage was the target missed?
Reasons: What factors are responsible for not meeting the projected target?</td></tr>
<tr><td colspan="5">Part B
Number of radical and incremental product innovation ideas generated in the skin-cleansing segment</td></tr>
<tr><td colspan="5">Radical: Number of radical innovation ideas generated during the period under review</td></tr>
<tr><td rowspan="2">Radical product innovation ideas generated in the skin-cleansing segment:
Was the target for this product category achieved? (check "Yes" or "No")</td><td>Yes</td><td>Comment</td><td>No</td><td>Comment</td></tr>
<tr><td></td><td>If yes, indicate the percentage achieved.
Reasons: What factors are responsible for achieving or exceeding the set target?</td><td></td><td>If no, by what percentage was the target missed?
Reasons: What factors are responsible for not meeting the projected target?</td></tr>
</table>

table continues on next page

<table>
<tr><td colspan="5">Incremental: Number of incremental innovation ideas generated during the period under review</td></tr>
<tr><td rowspan="2">Incremental product innovation ideas generated in the skin-cleansing segment:
Was the target for this product category achieved? (check "Yes" or "No")</td><td>Yes</td><td>Comment</td><td>No</td><td>Comment</td></tr>
<tr><td></td><td>If yes, indicate the percentage achieved.
Reasons: What factors are responsible for achieving or exceeding the set target?</td><td></td><td>If no, by what percentage was the target missed?
Reasons: What factors are responsible for not meeting the projected target?</td></tr>
<tr><td colspan="5">Part C
Number of radical and incremental product innovation ideas generated in the hair-care segment</td></tr>
<tr><td colspan="5">Radical: Number of radical innovation ideas generated during the period under review</td></tr>
<tr><td rowspan="2">Radical product innovation ideas generated in the hair-care segment:
Was the target for this product category achieved? (check "Yes" or "No")</td><td>Yes</td><td>Comment</td><td>No</td><td>Comment</td></tr>
<tr><td></td><td>If yes, indicate the percentage achieved.
Reasons: What factors are responsible for achieving or exceeding the set target?</td><td></td><td>If no, by what percentage was the target missed?
Reasons: What factors are responsible for not meeting the projected target?</td></tr>
</table>

table continues on next page

Incremental: **Number of incremental innovation ideas generated during the period under review**				
Incremental product innovation ideas generated in the hair-care segment: *Was the target for this product category achieved?* (check "Yes" or "No")	**Yes**	**Comment**	**No**	**Comment**
		If yes, indicate the percentage achieved. **Reasons:** *What factors are responsible for achieving or exceeding the set target?*		If no, by what percentage was the target missed? **Reasons:** *What factors are responsible for not meeting the projected target?*
Part D **Number of *radical* and *incremental* product innovation ideas generated in the hand-washing segment**				
Radical: **Number of radical innovation ideas generated during the period under review**				
Radical product innovation ideas generated in the hand-washing segment: *Was the target for this product category achieved?* (check "Yes" or "No")	**Yes**	**Comment**	**No**	**Comment**
		If yes, indicate the percentage achieved. **Reasons:** *What factors are responsible for achieving or exceeding the set target?*		If no, by what percentage was the target missed? **Reasons:** *What factors are responsible for not meeting the projected target?*

table continues on next page

Incremental: **Number of incremental innovation ideas generated during the period under review**				
Incremental product innovation ideas generated in the hand-washing segment: *Was the target for this product category achieved?* (check "Yes" or "No")	**Yes**	**Comment**	**No**	**Comment**
		If yes, indicate the percentage achieved. **Reasons:** *What factors are responsible for achieving or exceeding the set target?*		If no, by what percentage was the target missed? **Reasons:** *What factors are responsible for not meeting the projected target?*

Table 2-8. Example of Innovation Output Evaluation for Marketing Innovation Ideas

<table>
<tr><td colspan="5">Name of Department: Marketing department
Date: April 30, 2021</td></tr>
<tr><td colspan="5">Purpose of evaluation: To assess whether the target or goal of generating a particular number of radical and incremental marketing innovation ideas during the period under review (e.g., January–April of 2021) was achieved
The worksheet is presented according to the functional components of the marketing department of DM Personal Care Products:
• Part A: Product delivery
• Part B: Pricing
• Part C: Product promotion
• Part D: New markets
• Part E: Packaging</td></tr>
<tr><td colspan="5" align="center">Part A (i)
Revenue generation–focused product-delivery innovation ideas</td></tr>
<tr><td colspan="5">Number of radical and incremental product-delivery innovation ideas generated during the period under review</td></tr>
<tr><td colspan="5">Radical: Number of radical product-delivery innovation ideas generated during the period under review</td></tr>
<tr><td rowspan="2">Was the target for this category achieved? (check “Yes” or “No”)</td><td>Yes</td><td>Comment</td><td>No</td><td>Comment</td></tr>
<tr><td></td><td>If yes, indicate the percentage achieved.
Reasons: What factors are responsible for achieving or exceeding the set target?</td><td></td><td>If no, by what percentage was the target missed?
Reasons: What factors are responsible for not meeting the projected target?</td></tr>
</table>

table continues on next page

<table>
<tr><td colspan="5">Incremental: Number of incremental product-delivery innovation ideas generated during the period under review</td></tr>
<tr><td rowspan="2">Was the target for this category achieved? (check "Yes" or "No")</td><td>Yes</td><td>Comment</td><td>No</td><td>Comment</td></tr>
<tr><td></td><td>If yes, indicate the percentage achieved.
Reasons: What factors are responsible for achieving or exceeding the set target?</td><td></td><td>If no, by what percentage was the target missed?
Reasons: What factors are responsible for not meeting the projected target?</td></tr>
<tr><td colspan="5">Part A (ii)
Cost saving–focused product-delivery innovation ideas</td></tr>
<tr><td colspan="5">Number of radical and incremental product-delivery cost-saving innovation ideas generated during the period under review</td></tr>
<tr><td colspan="5">Radical: Number of radical product-delivery cost-saving innovation ideas generated during the period under review</td></tr>
<tr><td rowspan="2">Was the target for this category achieved? (check "Yes" or "No")</td><td>Yes</td><td>Comment</td><td>No</td><td>Comment</td></tr>
<tr><td></td><td>If yes, indicate the percentage achieved.
Reasons: What factors are responsible for achieving or exceeding the set target?</td><td></td><td>If no, by what percentage was the target missed?
Reasons: What factors are responsible for not meeting the projected target?</td></tr>
</table>

table continues on next page

<table>
<tr><td colspan="5">Incremental: Number of incremental product-delivery cost-saving innovation ideas generated during the period under review</td></tr>
<tr><td rowspan="2">Was the target for this category achieved? (check “Yes” or “No”)</td><td>Yes</td><td>Comment</td><td>No</td><td>Comment</td></tr>
<tr><td></td><td>If yes, indicate the percentage achieved.
Reasons: What factors are responsible for achieving or exceeding the set target?</td><td></td><td>If no, by what percentage was the target missed?
Reasons: What factors are responsible for not meeting the projected target?</td></tr>
<tr><td colspan="5">Part B
Pricing innovation ideas (for existing products)</td></tr>
<tr><td colspan="5">Number of radical and incremental pricing innovation ideas generated for existing products during the period under review</td></tr>
<tr><td colspan="5">Radical: Number of radical pricing innovation ideas generated for existing products during the period under review</td></tr>
<tr><td rowspan="2">Was the target for this category achieved? (check “Yes” or “No”)</td><td>Yes</td><td>Comment</td><td>No</td><td>Comment</td></tr>
<tr><td></td><td>If yes, indicate the percentage achieved.
Reasons: What factors are responsible for achieving or exceeding the set target?</td><td></td><td>If no, by what percentage was the target missed?
Reasons: What factors are responsible for not meeting the projected target?</td></tr>
</table>

table continues on next page

<table>
<tr><td colspan="5">Incremental: Number of incremental pricing innovation ideas generated for existing products during the period under review</td></tr>
<tr><td rowspan="2">Was the target for this category achieved? (check "Yes" or "No")</td><td>Yes</td><td>Comment</td><td>No</td><td>Comment</td></tr>
<tr><td></td><td>If yes, indicate the percentage achieved.

Reasons: What factors are responsible for achieving or exceeding the set target?</td><td></td><td>If no, by what percentage was the target missed?

Reasons: What factors are responsible for not meeting the projected target?</td></tr>
<tr><td colspan="5">Part C (i)

Revenue generation–focused product-promotion innovation ideas</td></tr>
<tr><td colspan="5">Number of radical and incremental product-promotion innovation ideas generated for existing products during the period under review</td></tr>
<tr><td colspan="5">Radical: Number of radical product-promotion innovation ideas generated for existing products during the period under review</td></tr>
<tr><td rowspan="2">Was the target for this category achieved? (check "Yes" or "No")</td><td>Yes</td><td>Comment</td><td>No</td><td>Comment</td></tr>
<tr><td></td><td>If yes, indicate the percentage achieved.

Reasons: What factors are responsible for achieving or exceeding the set target?</td><td></td><td>If no, by what percentage was the target missed?

Reasons: What factors are responsible for not meeting the projected target?</td></tr>
</table>

table continues on next page

<table>
<tr><td colspan="5">Incremental: Number of incremental product-promotion innovation ideas generated for existing products during the period under review</td></tr>
<tr><td rowspan="2">Was the target for this category achieved? (check "Yes" or "No")</td><td>Yes</td><td>Comment</td><td>No</td><td>Comment</td></tr>
<tr><td></td><td>If yes, indicate the percentage achieved.
Reasons: What factors are responsible for achieving or exceeding the set target?</td><td></td><td>If no, by what percentage was the target missed?
Reasons: What factors are responsible for not meeting the projected target?</td></tr>
<tr><td colspan="5">Part C (ii)
Cost saving–focused product-promotion innovation ideas</td></tr>
<tr><td colspan="5">Number of radical and incremental product-promotion cost-saving innovation ideas generated for existing products during the period under review</td></tr>
<tr><td colspan="5">Radical: Number of radical product-promotion cost-saving innovation ideas generated for existing products during the period under review</td></tr>
<tr><td rowspan="2">Was the target for this category achieved? (check "Yes" or "No")</td><td>Yes</td><td>Comment</td><td>No</td><td>Comment</td></tr>
<tr><td></td><td>If yes, indicate the percentage achieved.
Reasons: What factors are responsible for achieving or exceeding the set target?</td><td></td><td>If no, by what percentage was the target missed?
Reasons: What factors are responsible for not meeting the projected target?</td></tr>
</table>

table continues on next page

<table>
<tr><td colspan="5">Incremental: Number of incremental product-promotion cost-saving innovation ideas generated for existing products during the period under review</td></tr>
<tr><td rowspan="2">Was the target for this category achieved? (check "Yes" or "No")</td><td>Yes</td><td>Comment</td><td>No</td><td>Comment</td></tr>
<tr><td></td><td>If yes, indicate the percentage achieved.

Reasons: What factors are responsible for achieving or exceeding the set target?</td><td></td><td>If no, by what percentage was the target missed?

Reasons: What factors are responsible for not meeting the projected target?</td></tr>
<tr><td colspan="5">Part D

New-market innovation ideas</td></tr>
<tr><td colspan="5">Number of new-unserved-market and new-market-segment innovation ideas generated during the period under review</td></tr>
<tr><td colspan="5">New-unserved-market ideas: Number of new-unserved-market ideas generated for existing products in geographical locations not served by competitors or the organization during the period under review</td></tr>
<tr><td rowspan="2">Was the target for this category achieved? (check "Yes" or "No")</td><td>Yes</td><td>Comment</td><td>No</td><td>Comment</td></tr>
<tr><td></td><td>If yes, indicate the percentage achieved.

Reasons: What factors are responsible for achieving or exceeding the set target?</td><td></td><td>If no, by what percentage was the target missed?

Reasons: What factors are responsible for not meeting the projected target?</td></tr>
</table>

table continues on next page

New-market-segment ideas: **Number of new-market-segment ideas generated for existing products within existing markets or geographical locations during the period under review**				
Was the target for this category achieved? (check "Yes" or "No")	**Yes**	**Comment**	**No**	**Comment**
		If yes, indicate the percentage achieved. **Reasons:** *What factors are responsible for achieving or exceeding the set target?*		If no, by what percentage was the target missed? **Reasons:** *What factors are responsible for not meeting the projected target?*
Part E (i) **Revenue generation–focused packaging innovation ideas**				
Number of *radical* and *incremental* packaging innovation ideas generated during the period under review				
Radical: **Number of radical packaging innovation ideas generated during the period under review**				
Was the target for this category achieved? (check "Yes" or "No")	**Yes**	**Comment**	**No**	**Comment**
		If yes, indicate the percentage achieved. **Reasons:** *What factors are responsible for achieving or exceeding the set target?*		If no, by what percentage was the target missed? **Reasons:** *What factors are responsible for not meeting the projected target?*

table continues on next page

<table>
<tr><td colspan="5">Incremental: Number of incremental packaging innovation ideas generated during the period under review</td></tr>
<tr><td rowspan="2">Was the target for this category achieved? (check "Yes" or "No")</td><td>Yes</td><td>Comment</td><td>No</td><td>Comment</td></tr>
<tr><td></td><td>If yes, indicate the percentage achieved.
Reasons: What factors are responsible for achieving or exceeding the set target?</td><td></td><td>If no, by what percentage was the target missed?
Reasons: What factors are responsible for not meeting the projected target?</td></tr>
<tr><td colspan="5">Part E (ii)
Cost-saving packaging innovation ideas</td></tr>
<tr><td colspan="5">Number of radical and incremental cost-saving packaging innovation ideas generated during the period under review</td></tr>
<tr><td colspan="5">Radical: Number of radical cost-saving packaging innovation ideas generated during the period under review</td></tr>
<tr><td rowspan="2">Was the target for this category achieved? (check "Yes" or "No")</td><td>Yes</td><td>Comment</td><td>No</td><td>Comment</td></tr>
<tr><td></td><td>If yes, indicate the percentage achieved.
Reasons: What factors are responsible for achieving or exceeding the set target?</td><td></td><td>If no, by what percentage was the target missed?
Reasons: What factors are responsible for not meeting the projected target?</td></tr>
</table>

table continues on next page

<table>
<tr><td colspan="5">Incremental: Number of incremental cost-saving packaging innovation ideas generated during the period under review</td></tr>
<tr><td rowspan="2">Was the target for this category achieved? (tick "Yes" or "No")</td><td>Yes</td><td>Comment</td><td>No</td><td>Comment</td></tr>
<tr><td></td><td>If yes, indicate the percentage achieved.
Reasons: What factors are responsible for achieving or exceeding the set target?</td><td></td><td>If no, by what percentage was the target missed?
Reasons: What factors are responsible for not meeting the projected target?</td></tr>
</table>

Table 2-7 and 2-8 show how the evaluation worksheet can be applied to two different core functional units (product development and marketing). Similarly, the evaluation worksheet can be applied to the other core functional units of DM Personal Care Products:

- Manufacturing-processes department
- Customer service department

Table 2-9 shows how the evaluation worksheet can be applied to the support functional units of DM Personal Care Products, using the procurement department as an example.

Table 2-9. Example of Innovation Output Evaluation for Cost-Saving Procurement Innovation Ideas

<table>
<tr><td colspan="5">Name of Department: Procurement
Date: April 30, 2021</td></tr>
<tr><td colspan="5">Purpose of evaluation: To assess whether the target or goal of generating a particular number of radical and incremental cost-saving procurement innovation ideas during the period under review (e.g., January–April of 2021) was achieved
This worksheet is divided into two parts:
Part A: Number of radical cost-saving procurement innovation ideas generated during the period under review
Part B: Number of incremental cost-saving procurement innovation ideas generated during the period under review</td></tr>
<tr><td colspan="5">Part A
Number of radical cost-saving procurement innovation ideas generated during the period under review</td></tr>
<tr><td rowspan="2">Was the target for this category achieved? (check “Yes” or “No”)</td><td>Yes</td><td>Comment</td><td>No</td><td>Comment</td></tr>
<tr><td></td><td>If yes, indicate the percentage achieved.
Reasons: What factors are responsible for achieving or exceeding the set target?</td><td></td><td>If no, by what percentage was the target missed?
Reasons: What factors are responsible for not meeting the projected target?</td></tr>
<tr><td colspan="5">Part B
Number of incremental cost-saving procurement innovation ideas generated during the period under review</td></tr>
<tr><td rowspan="2">Was the target for this category achieved? (check “Yes” or “No”)</td><td>Yes</td><td>Comment</td><td>No</td><td>Comment</td></tr>
<tr><td></td><td>If yes, indicate the percentage achieved.
Reasons: What factors are responsible for achieving or exceeding the set target?</td><td></td><td>If no, by what percentage was the target missed?
Reasons: What factors are responsible for not meeting the projected target?</td></tr>
</table>

As with the previous two tables, Table 2-9 can also be applied to the other support functional units of DM Personal Care Products to assess the number of cost-saving innovation ideas generated:

- HR department
- Finance and accounting department
- IT department
- Corporate affairs department

Innovation Output Evaluation for Ideas Undergoing Development

The second type of output evaluation is the innovation output evaluation for ideas undergoing development.

Just as it is important to assess the number of ideas generated, it is necessary to assess whether the target or goal of having a particular number of ideas undergoing development in the core and support functional units of DM Personal Care Products over a particular period was achieved. Tables 2-10 through 2-12 show how the innovation output evaluation worksheet is applied to assessing the number of innovation ideas undergoing development over a particular period. For illustration purposes, the evaluation worksheet is applied to three functional units: the product-development unit (Table 2-10), the marketing department (Table 2-11), and the procurement department (Table 2-12).

Table 2-10. Example of Innovation Output Evaluation for Product Innovation Ideas Undergoing Development

<table>
<tr><td colspan="5">Name of Department: Product-development unit
Date: April 30, 2021</td></tr>
<tr><td colspan="5">Purpose of evaluation: To assess whether the target or goal of having a particular number of radical and incremental product innovation ideas undergoing development during the period under review (e.g., January–April of 2021) was achieved
The worksheet is divided into the four product segments of the product-development unit of DM Personal Care Products:
• Part A: Body-lotions segment
• Part B: Skin-cleansing segment
• Part C: Hair-care segment
• Part D: Hand-washing segment</td></tr>
<tr><td colspan="5">Part A
Number of radical and incremental innovation ideas undergoing development in the body-lotions segment</td></tr>
<tr><td colspan="5">Radical: Number of radical innovation ideas in the body-lotions segment undergoing development during the period under review</td></tr>
<tr><td rowspan="2">Radical innovation ideas undergoing development in the body-lotions segment:
Was the target for this product category achieved? (check "Yes" or "No")</td><td>Yes</td><td>Comment</td><td>No</td><td>Comment</td></tr>
<tr><td></td><td>If yes, indicate the percentage achieved.
Reasons: What factors are responsible for achieving or exceeding the set target?</td><td></td><td>If no, by what percentage was the target missed?
Reasons: What factors are responsible for not meeting the projected target?</td></tr>
</table>

table continues on next page

<table>
<tr><td colspan="5">Incremental: Number of incremental innovation ideas in the body-lotions segment undergoing development during the period under review</td></tr>
<tr><td rowspan="2">Incremental innovation ideas undergoing development in the body-lotions segment:
Was the target for this product category achieved? (check “Yes” or “No”)</td><td>Yes</td><td>Comment</td><td>No</td><td>Comment</td></tr>
<tr><td></td><td>If yes, indicate the percentage achieved.
Reasons: What factors are responsible for achieving or exceeding the set target?</td><td></td><td>If no, by what percentage was the target missed?
Reasons: What factors are responsible for not meeting the projected target?</td></tr>
<tr><td colspan="5">Part B
Number of radical and incremental product innovation ideas undergoing development in the skin-cleansing segment</td></tr>
<tr><td colspan="5">Radical: Number of radical innovation ideas undergoing development in the skin-cleansing segment during the period under review</td></tr>
<tr><td rowspan="2">Radical product innovation ideas undergoing development in the skin-cleansing segment:
Was the target for this product category achieved? (check “Yes” or “No”)</td><td>Yes</td><td>Comment</td><td>No</td><td>Comment</td></tr>
<tr><td></td><td>If yes, indicate the percentage achieved.
Reasons: What factors are responsible for achieving or exceeding the set target?</td><td></td><td>If no, by what percentage was the target missed?
Reasons: What factors are responsible for not meeting the projected target?</td></tr>
</table>

table continues on next page

Incremental: **Number of incremental innovation ideas undergoing development in the skin-cleansing segment during the period under review**				
Incremental product innovation ideas undergoing development in the skin-cleansing segment: *Was the target for this product category achieved?* (tick "Yes" or "No")	**Yes**	**Comment**	**No**	**Comment**
		If yes, indicate the percentage achieved. **Reasons:** *What factors are responsible for achieving or exceeding the set target?*		If no, by what percentage was the target missed? **Reasons:** *What factors are responsible for not meeting the projected target?*
Part C **Number of *radical* and *incremental* product innovation ideas undergoing development in the hair-care segment**				
Radical: **Number of radical innovation ideas undergoing development in the hair-care segment during the period under review**				
Radical product innovation ideas undergoing development in the hair-care segment: *Was the target for this product category achieved?* (check "Yes" or "No")	**Yes**	**Comment**	**No**	**Comment**
		If yes, indicate the percentage achieved. **Reasons:** *What factors are responsible for achieving or exceeding the set target?*		If no, by what percentage was the target missed? **Reasons:** *What factors are responsible for not meeting the projected target?*

table continues on next page

<table>
<tr><td colspan="5">Incremental: Number of incremental innovation ideas undergoing development in the hair-care segment during the period under review</td></tr>
<tr><td rowspan="2">Incremental product innovation ideas undergoing development in the hair-care segment:
Was the target for this product category achieved? (check “Yes” or “No”)</td><td>Yes</td><td>Comment</td><td>No</td><td>Comment</td></tr>
<tr><td></td><td>If yes, indicate the percentage achieved.
Reasons: What factors are responsible for achieving or exceeding the set target?</td><td></td><td>If no, by what percentage was the target missed?
Reasons: What factors are responsible for not meeting the projected target?</td></tr>
<tr><td colspan="5">Part D
Number of radical and incremental product innovation ideas undergoing development in the hand-washing segment</td></tr>
<tr><td colspan="5">Radical: Number of radical innovation ideas undergoing development in the hand-washing segment during the period under review</td></tr>
<tr><td rowspan="2">Radical product innovation ideas undergoing development in the hand-washing segment:
Was the target for this product category achieved? (check “Yes” or “No”)</td><td>Yes</td><td>Comment</td><td>No</td><td>Comment</td></tr>
<tr><td></td><td>If yes, indicate the percentage achieved.
Reasons: What factors are responsible for achieving or exceeding the set target?</td><td></td><td>If no, by what percentage was the target missed?
Reasons: What factors are responsible for not meeting the projected target?</td></tr>
</table>

table continues on next page

<table>
<tr><td colspan="5">Incremental: Number of incremental innovation ideas undergoing development in the hand-washing segment during the period under review</td></tr>
<tr><td rowspan="2">Incremental product innovation ideas undergoing development in the hand-washing segment:
Was the target for this product category achieved? (tick "Yes" or "No")</td><td>Yes</td><td>Comment</td><td>No</td><td>Comment</td></tr>
<tr><td></td><td>If yes, indicate the percentage achieved.
Reasons: What factors are responsible for achieving or exceeding the set target?</td><td></td><td>If no, by what percentage was the target missed?
Reasons: What factors are responsible for not meeting the projected target?</td></tr>
</table>

Table 2-10. Example of Innovation Output Evaluation for Marketing Innovation Ideas Undergoing Development

<table>
<tr><td colspan="5">Name of Department: Marketing department
Date: April 30, 2021</td></tr>
<tr><td colspan="5">Purpose of evaluation: To assess whether the target or goal of having a particular number of marketing innovation ideas undergoing development during the period under review (e.g., January–April of 2021) was achieved
The worksheet is divided into the functional components of the marketing department of DM Personal Care Products:
• Part A: Product delivery
• Part B: Pricing
• Part C: Product promotion
• Part D: New markets
• Part E: Packaging</td></tr>
<tr><td colspan="5">Part A (i)
Revenue generation–focused product-delivery innovation ideas</td></tr>
<tr><td colspan="5">Number of radical and incremental product-delivery innovation ideas undergoing development during the period under review</td></tr>
<tr><td colspan="5">Radical: Number of radical product-delivery innovation ideas undergoing development during the period under review</td></tr>
<tr><td rowspan="2">Was the target for this category achieved? (check “Yes” or “No”)</td><td>Yes</td><td>Comment</td><td>No</td><td>Comment</td></tr>
<tr><td></td><td>If yes, indicate the percentage achieved.
Reasons: What factors are responsible for achieving or exceeding the set target?</td><td></td><td>If no, by what percentage was the target missed?
Reasons: What factors are responsible for not meeting the projected target?</td></tr>
</table>

table continues on next page

<table>
<tr><td colspan="5">Incremental: Number of incremental product-delivery innovation ideas undergoing development during the period under review</td></tr>
<tr><td rowspan="2">Was the target for this category achieved? (tick "Yes" or "No")</td><td>Yes</td><td>Comment</td><td>No</td><td>Comment</td></tr>
<tr><td></td><td>If yes, indicate the percentage achieved.

Reasons: What factors are responsible for achieving or exceeding the set target?</td><td></td><td>If no, by what percentage was the target missed?

Reasons: What factors are responsible for not meeting the projected target?</td></tr>
<tr><td colspan="5">Part A (ii)

Cost saving–focused product-delivery innovation ideas</td></tr>
<tr><td colspan="5">Number of radical and incremental product-delivery cost-saving innovation ideas undergoing development during the period under review</td></tr>
<tr><td colspan="5">Radical: Number of radical product-delivery cost-saving innovation ideas undergoing development during the period under review</td></tr>
<tr><td rowspan="2">Was the target for this category achieved? (check "Yes" or "No")</td><td>Yes</td><td>Comment</td><td>No</td><td>Comment</td></tr>
<tr><td></td><td>If yes, indicate the percentage achieved.

Reasons: What factors are responsible for achieving or exceeding the set target?</td><td></td><td>If no, by what percentage was the target missed?

Reasons: What factors are responsible for not meeting the projected target?</td></tr>
</table>

table continues on next page

Incremental: **Number of incremental product-delivery cost-saving innovation ideas undergoing development during the period under review**				
Was the target for this category achieved? (check "Yes" or "No")	**Yes**	**Comment**	**No**	**Comment**
		If yes, indicate the percentage achieved. **Reasons:** *What factors are responsible for achieving or exceeding the set target?*		If no, by what percentage was the target missed? **Reasons:** *What factors are responsible for not meeting the projected target?*
Part B **Pricing innovation ideas** *(for existing products)*				
Number of *radical* and *incremental* pricing innovation ideas undergoing development for existing products during the period under review				
Radical: **Number of radical pricing innovation ideas undergoing development for existing products during the period under review**				
Was the target for this category achieved? (check "Yes" or "No")	**Yes**	**Comment**	**No**	**Comment**
		If yes, indicate the percentage achieved. **Reasons:** *What factors are responsible for achieving or exceeding the set target?*		If no, by what percentage was the target missed? **Reasons:** *What factors are responsible for not meeting the projected target?*

table continues on next page

<table>
<tr><td colspan="5">Incremental: Number of incremental pricing innovation ideas undergoing development for existing products during the period under review</td></tr>
<tr><td rowspan="2">Was the target for this category achieved? (check "Yes" or "No")</td><td>Yes</td><td>Comment</td><td>No</td><td>Comment</td></tr>
<tr><td></td><td>If yes, indicate the percentage achieved.
Reasons: What factors are responsible for achieving or exceeding the set target?</td><td></td><td>If no, by what percentage was the target missed?
Reasons: What factors are responsible for not meeting the projected target?</td></tr>
<tr><td colspan="5">Part C (i)
Revenue generation–focused product-promotion innovation ideas</td></tr>
<tr><td colspan="5">Number of radical and incremental product-promotion innovation ideas undergoing development for existing products during the period under review</td></tr>
<tr><td colspan="5">Radical: Number of radical product-promotion innovation ideas undergoing development for existing products during the period under review</td></tr>
<tr><td rowspan="2">Was the target for this category achieved? (check "Yes" or "No")</td><td>Yes</td><td>Comment</td><td>No</td><td>Comment</td></tr>
<tr><td></td><td>If yes, indicate the percentage achieved.
Reasons: What factors are responsible for achieving or exceeding the set target?</td><td></td><td>If no, by what percentage was the target missed?
Reasons: What factors are responsible for not meeting the projected target?</td></tr>
</table>

table continues on next page

<table>
<tr><td colspan="5">Incremental: Number of incremental product-promotion innovation ideas undergoing development for existing products during the period under review</td></tr>
<tr><td rowspan="2">Was the target for this category achieved? (check "Yes" or "No")</td><td>Yes</td><td>Comment</td><td>No</td><td>Comment</td></tr>
<tr><td></td><td>If yes, indicate the percentage achieved.
Reasons: What factors are responsible for achieving or exceeding the set target?</td><td></td><td>If no, by what percentage was the target missed?
Reasons: What factors are responsible for not meeting the projected target?</td></tr>
<tr><td colspan="5">Part C (ii)
Cost saving–focused product-promotion innovation ideas</td></tr>
<tr><td colspan="5">Number of radical and incremental product-promotion cost-saving innovation ideas undergoing development for existing products during the period under review</td></tr>
<tr><td colspan="5">Radical: Number of radical product-promotion cost-saving innovation ideas undergoing development for existing products during the period under review</td></tr>
<tr><td rowspan="2">Was the target for this category achieved? (check "Yes" or "No")</td><td>Yes</td><td>Comment</td><td>No</td><td>Comment</td></tr>
<tr><td></td><td>If yes, indicate the percentage achieved.
Reasons: What factors are responsible for achieving or exceeding the set target?</td><td></td><td>If no, by what percentage was the target missed?
Reasons: What factors are responsible for not meeting the projected target?</td></tr>
</table>

table continues on next page

Incremental: **Number of incremental product-promotion cost-saving innovation ideas undergoing development for existing products during the period under review**				
Was the target for this category achieved? (check "Yes" or "No")	**Yes**	**Comment**	**No**	**Comment**
		If yes, indicate the percentage achieved. **Reasons:** *What factors are responsible for achieving or exceeding the set target?*		If no, by what percentage was the target missed? **Reasons:** *What factors are responsible for not meeting the projected target?*
Part D **New-market innovation ideas**				
Number of *new-unserved-market* and *new-market-segment* innovation ideas undergoing development during the period under review				
New-unserved-market ideas: **Number of new-unserved-market ideas undergoing development for existing products in geographical locations not served by competitors or the organization during the period under review**				
Was the target for this category achieved? (check "Yes" or "No")	**Yes**	**Comment**	**No**	**Comment**
		If yes, indicate the percentage achieved. **Reasons:** *What factors are responsible for achieving or exceeding the set target?*		If no, by what percentage was the target missed? **Reasons:** *What factors are responsible for not meeting the projected target?*

table continues on next page

<table>
<tr><td colspan="5">New-market-segment ideas: Number of new-market-segment ideas undergoing development for existing products within existing markets or geographical locations during the period under review</td></tr>
<tr><td rowspan="2">Was the target for this category achieved? (tick "Yes" or "No")</td><td>Yes</td><td>Comment</td><td>No</td><td>Comment</td></tr>
<tr><td></td><td>If yes, indicate the percentage achieved.
Reasons: What factors are responsible for achieving or exceeding the set target?</td><td></td><td>If no, by what percentage was the target missed?
Reasons: What factors are responsible for not meeting the projected target?</td></tr>
<tr><td colspan="5">Part E(i)
Revenue generation–focused packaging innovation ideas</td></tr>
<tr><td colspan="5">Number of radical and incremental packaging innovation ideas undergoing development during the period under review</td></tr>
<tr><td colspan="5">Radical: Number of radical packaging innovation ideas undergoing development during the period under review</td></tr>
<tr><td rowspan="2">Was the target for this category achieved? (check "Yes" or "No")</td><td>Yes</td><td>Comment</td><td>No</td><td>Comment</td></tr>
<tr><td></td><td>If yes, indicate the percentage achieved.
Reasons: What factors are responsible for achieving or exceeding the set target?</td><td></td><td>If no, by what percentage was the target missed?
Reasons: What factors are responsible for not meeting the projected target?</td></tr>
</table>

table continues on next page

<table>
<tr><td colspan="5">Incremental: Number of incremental packaging innovation ideas undergoing development during the period under review</td></tr>
<tr><td rowspan="2">Was the target for this category achieved? (check "Yes" or "No")</td><td>Yes</td><td>Comment</td><td>No</td><td>Comment</td></tr>
<tr><td></td><td>If yes, indicate the percentage achieved.
Reasons: What factors are responsible for achieving or exceeding the set target?</td><td></td><td>If no, by what percentage was the target missed?
Reasons: What factors are responsible for not meeting the projected target?</td></tr>
<tr><td colspan="5">Part F (ii)
Cost-saving packaging innovation ideas</td></tr>
<tr><td colspan="5">Number of radical and incremental cost-saving packaging innovation ideas undergoing development during the period under review</td></tr>
<tr><td colspan="5">Radical: Number of radical cost-saving packaging innovation ideas undergoing development during the period under review</td></tr>
<tr><td rowspan="2">Was the target for this category achieved? (check "Yes" or "No")</td><td>Yes</td><td>Comment</td><td>No</td><td>Comment</td></tr>
<tr><td></td><td>If yes, indicate the percentage achieved.
Reasons: What factors are responsible for achieving or exceeding the set target?</td><td></td><td>If no, by what percentage was the target missed?
Reasons: What factors are responsible for not meeting the projected target?</td></tr>
</table>

table continues on next page

Incremental: **Number of incremental cost-saving packaging innovation ideas undergoing development during the period under review**				
Was the target for this category achieved? (check "Yes" or "No")	**Yes**	**Comment**	**No**	**Comment**
		If yes, indicate the percentage achieved. **Reasons:** *What factors are responsible for achieving or exceeding the set target?*		If no, by what percentage was the target missed? **Reasons:** *What factors are responsible for not meeting the projected target?*

The evaluation worksheet format shown in Tables 2-10 and 2-11 can similarly be applied to the other core functional units of DM Personal Care Products:

- Manufacturing-processes department
- Customer service department

Tables 2-12 shows the format of the evaluation worksheet as applied to one of the support functional units of DM Personal Care Products, the procurement department.

Table 2-12. Example of Innovation Output Evaluation for Cost-Saving Procurement Innovation Ideas Undergoing Development

<table>
<tr><td colspan="5">Name of Department: Procurement department

Date: April 30, 2021</td></tr>
<tr><td colspan="5">Purpose of Evaluation: To assess whether the target or goal of having a particular number of radical and incremental cost-saving procurement innovation ideas undergoing development during the period under review (e.g., January–April of 2021) was achieved

The worksheet is divided into two parts:

Part A: Number of radical cost-saving procurement innovation ideas undergoing development during the period under review

Part B: Number of incremental cost-saving procurement innovation ideas undergoing development during the period under review</td></tr>
<tr><td colspan="5">Part A

Number of radical cost-saving procurement innovation ideas undergoing development during the period under review</td></tr>
<tr><td rowspan="2">Was the target for this category achieved? (check “Yes” or “No”)</td><td>Yes</td><td>Comment</td><td>No</td><td>Comment</td></tr>
<tr><td></td><td>If yes, indicate the percentage achieved.

Reasons: What factors are responsible for achieving or exceeding the set target?</td><td></td><td>If no, by what percentage was the target missed?

Reasons: What factors are responsible for not meeting the projected target?</td></tr>
</table>

table continues on next page

Part B **Number of incremental cost-saving procurement innovation ideas undergoing development during the period under review**				
Was the target for this category achieved? (check "Yes" or "No")	**Yes**	**Comment**	**No**	**Comment**
		If yes, indicate the percentage achieved. **Reasons:** *What factors are responsible for achieving or exceeding the set target?*		If no, by what percentage was the target missed? **Reasons:** *What factors are responsible for not meeting the projected target?*

As with the previous tables, the evaluation worksheet format shown in Table 2-12 can similarly be applied to the other support functional units of DM Personal Care Products to assess the number of cost-saving innovation ideas undergoing development:

- HR department
- Finance and accounting department
- IT department
- Corporate affairs department

Having concluded the section on innovation output measurement, we now turn to innovation-results measurement.

Step Three

INNOVATION-RESULTS MEASUREMENT

Overview

So far, we've looked at two metrics of measuring innovation performance: innovation input measurement and innovation output measurement. The third metric of measuring innovation performance is *innovation-results measurement*. Step Three covers (1) definitions (2) aspects to consider (3) Illustration: how to present innovation-results measurement (4) New-markets unit: characterizing innovation in the context of new markets? (5) Innovation-results evaluation worksheet

Definitions

To understand innovation-results measurement, it is first necessary to grasp the meaning of the term. According to the *Merriam-Webster* online dictionary, the word *result* means "a final consequence of a sequence of actions or events expressed qualitatively or quantitatively."

In the context of innovation, the interpretation of *innovation results* is a series of consequences of innovation management–related actions and activities. Normally, innovation ideas go through an assessment process that leads to the conversion of the innovation ideas into innovations. So, an innovation is essentially the end product or end result of an innovation idea that has proceeded through a rigorous development process. So, what does the term *innovation results* mean?

Definition of *Innovation Results*

This book's definition of *innovation results* is based on two things: first, that innovations are an end product of innovation ideas, and second, that the basic meaning of the word *results* is "a final consequence of a sequence of actions and activities." Thus, this book defines *innovation results* as a resultant end product of the innovation-idea assessment and development processes in the context of a particular type of innovation and innovation degree.

Definition of *Innovation-Results Measurement*

Given the meaning of the term *innovation results*, this book defines *innovation-results measurement* as a process that involves determining whether the intended final resultant end product of the development or conversion process of an innovation idea was realized.

Having covered what innovation results entail, we now turn to the pertinent aspects of innovation-results measurements, which include the following:

- Aspects to consider when undertaking innovation-results measurement
- How to present innovation-results measurement
- Formulating an innovation-results evaluation worksheet

Aspects to Consider

The earlier discussion of innovation output measurement stated some important aspects and practices to take into account when compiling an organization's innovation-performance report. Similar considerations apply to innovation-results measurement, although in a different context. The aspects and practices are as follows:

- *Collaboration between various innovation-idea management committees, functional leaders, and teams responsible for compiling innovation-performance reports:* This is helpful in terms of ascertaining the number of innovations developed and, in some cases, patents obtained during the period under review.
- *Presentation format:* Generally, one of the purposes of reporting innovation performance in organizations is to enable every person in the organization, from the CEO to the most junior employee, to understand how the organization is faring in all critical elements of its innovation practices. Therefore, using the wrong presentation format will impair the process of reporting innovation performance. For this reason, the leadership should ensure that the presentation format used is simple, creative, and interesting so that audiences across functional units understand every aspect of the data presented on innovations launched or implemented.

Illustration:
How to Present Innovation-Results Measurement

As in previous sections, this section uses the functional units of DM Personal Care Products to illustrate how to present innovations launched or implemented.

However, before beginning the example, it's important to remember some of the steps mentioned when outlining how to present data on the number of innovation ideas generated. Similar steps should be observed when determining innovations launched or implemented. The three steps are as follows:

- Identify the core and support functional units of the company
- Select a presentation format for the report that is structured according to the functional units or divisions of the company

- In terms of determining the number of product innovations launched, categorize the presentation according to the company's product platforms

An example of how these steps can be applied to present the innovations launched or implemented across the functional units of DM Personal Care Products is presented next.

Outline of Functional Units

Recall that the functional units of DM Personal Care Products are as follows:

Core functional units

- Product-development unit, with the following segments:
  - Body-lotions segment
  - Skin-cleansing segment
  - Hair-care segment
  - Hand-washing segment
- Manufacturing-processes department
- Marketing department, with the following units:
  - Pricing unit
  - Product-promotion unit
  - Product-delivery unit
  - New-markets unit
  - Packaging unit
- Customer service department

Support functional units

- Procurement department
- HR department
- Finance and accounting department
- IT department
- Corporate affairs department

Presentation Format

As in previous sections, simple charts are used to show how to present the number of radical and incremental innovations launched or implemented over a particular period in each of the core and support functional units of DM Personal Care Products. As with previous examples, the innovation results of the core functional units are presented first, followed by those for the support units.

Product-Development Department

The number of radical and incremental product innovations launched in the product-development functional unit over a particular period is presented for each of the four product categories:

- Body-lotions category
- Skin-cleansing category
- Hair-care category
- Hand-washing category

Figures 3-21 and 3-22 show the number of radical and incremental body-lotion innovations launched in each quarter of 2021 (target and actual).

Figure 3-21

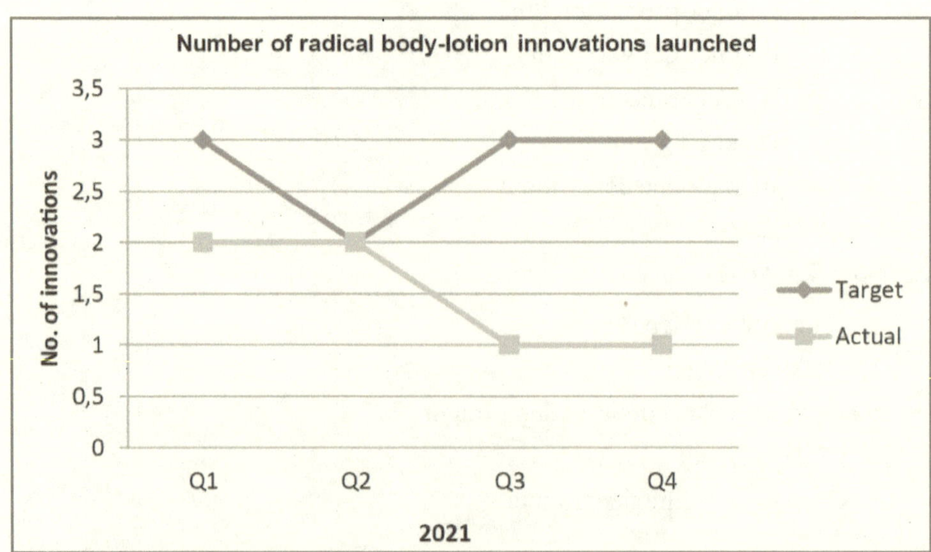

Figure 3-22

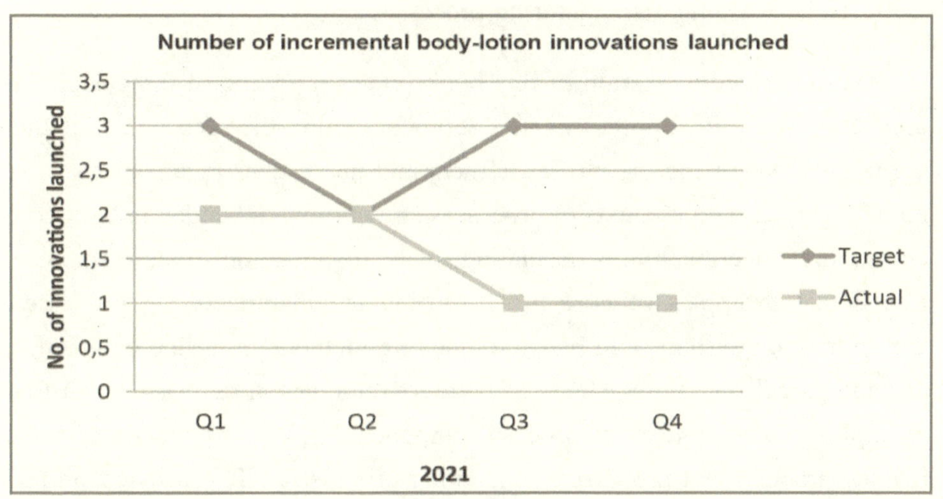

Similar charts would be created to present the number of radical and incremental innovations launched in each of the other three product categories over the same period:

- Skin-cleansing category
- Hair-care category
- Hand-washing category

As stated in the earlier section on determining innovation ideas, in some instances, a product category may have a number of product segments; in such cases, the number of radical and incremental innovations launched should be determined per each product segment of a particular product category.

Manufacturing-Processes Department

The second example shows how to present innovation-results measurement for the manufacturing department. Recall that this functional unit has four main manufacturing-processes categories:

- Body-lotions manufacturing-processes category
- Skin-cleansing manufacturing-processes category

- Hair-care manufacturing-processes category
- Hand-washing manufacturing-processes category

The Introduction section of this book (under the topic of dimensions of innovation) described processes as a series of behind-the-scenes actions that are usually out of the view of customers and noted that organizations have numerous types and contexts of processes structurally embedded in their core and support functional units depending on the organization's nature and size. Recall that examples of core processes include manufacturing processes, the reservation systems and baggage-tracking methods in airline companies, and the parcel-tracking systems of couriers, among others. Also recall that examples of the contexts of process components in support functional units include procurement processes, accounting processes, HR processes, and so forth. Thus, process activities and components vary from company to company depending on the type and nature of the company and differ across industries.

Manufacturing processes are the behind-the-scenes series of operations or collections of technologies and methods that are used, performed, or applied when making a product in a manufacturing facility. Thus, manufacturing-processes innovations can include things like innovative procedures or technologies aimed at enhancing production processes in terms of the following: quality of the product, time of production, ability to customize the production process within a short time, ability to produce at low cost, ability to produce in large numbers without compromising on quality, and improvements in packaging methods or assembly methods.

That said, the charts in figures 3-23 and 3-24 provide an example of how to present the number of radical and incremental manufacturing-processes innovations in the manufacturing-processes categories of DM Personal Care Products. Specifically, figures 3-23 and 3-24 show the number of radical and incremental body-lotions manufacturing-processes innovations implemented in each quarter of 2021 (target and actual).

Figure 3-23

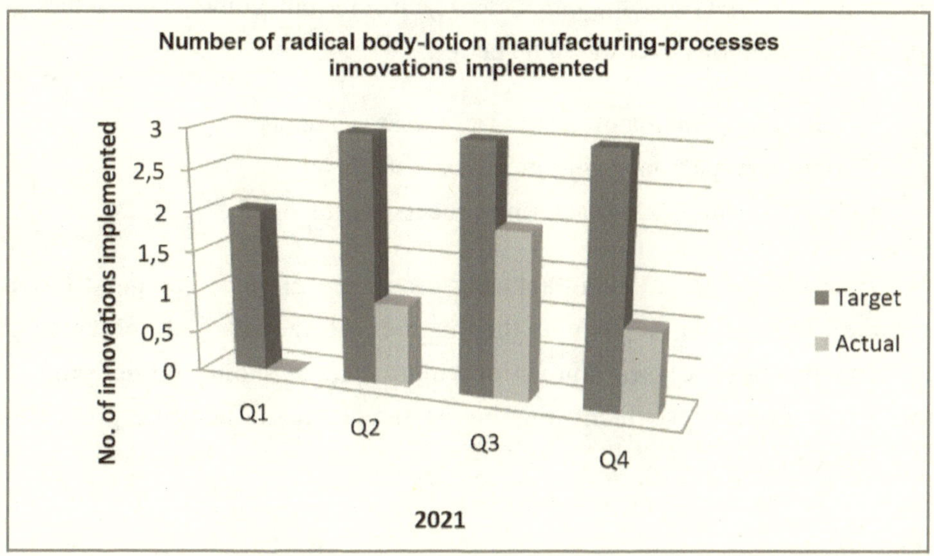

Figure 3-24

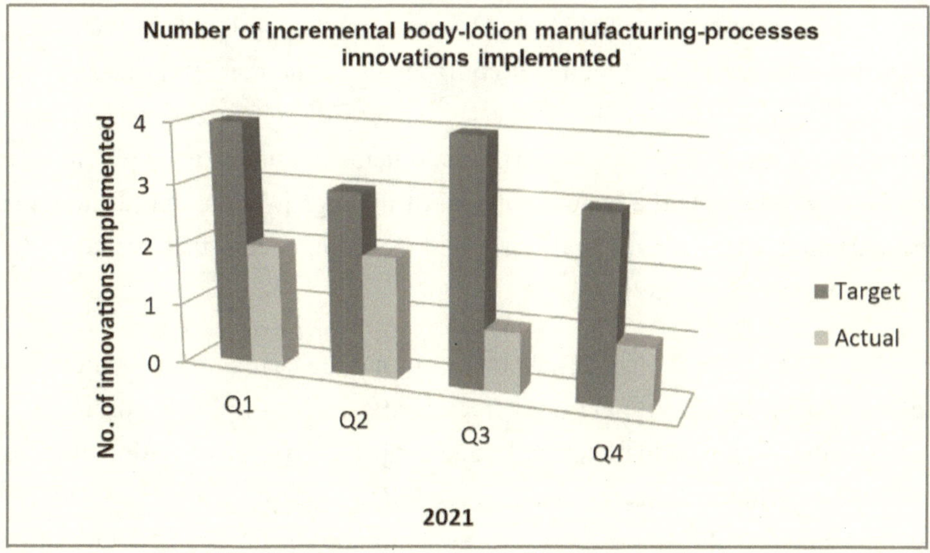

Similar charts would be created to show the number of radical and incremental innovations implemented in each of the other three manufacturing-processes categories over the same period:

- Skin-cleansing manufacturing-processes category
- Hair-care manufacturing-processes category
- Hand-washing manufacturing-processes category

In cases where a manufacturing-processes product category has a number of product segments, the number of radical and incremental manufacturing-processes innovations implemented should be determined per each product segment of the particular manufacturing-processes product category.

Marketing Department

The discussion of dimensions of innovation in chapter 8 stated that *marketing innovation* is a general term that describes the generation and development of innovative marketing-related ideas. However, marketing is a very wide area, and the structure of the functional components of the marketing department is usually determined by the nature and size of the organization. Similarly, the type of marketing innovation ideas generated usually depends (among other aspects) on (1) the business model of the organization and (2) how the organization characterizes and describes the components that make up its marketing functional unit.

For DM Personal Care Products, recall that the segments or components of the marketing department are categorized as pricing, product promotion, product delivery, new markets, and packaging. Thus, the presentation of types of marketing innovations is organized according to these marketing functional components. For illustration purposes, the continuing example will demonstrate how to present two types of marketing-related innovations: *number of product-promotion innovations launched* and *number of new markets discovered.*

Presenting the Number of Radical and Incremental Product-Promotion Innovations Launched

There are two categories of product-promotion innovations. Category 1 is *revenue-focused product-promotion innovations*—that is, product-promotion innovations that result in attracting revenue for the company. Category 2 is *cost saving–focused product-promotion innovations*—that is, product-promotion innovations that are aimed at cutting *product promotion–related costs*.

Presentation Format

The charts in figures 3-25 through 3-26 show product-promotion innovations launched in categories 1 and 2.

Figures 3-25 and 3-26 show the number of radical and incremental revenue-focused product-promotion innovations (category 1) launched in each quarter of 2021 (target and actual).

Figure 3-25

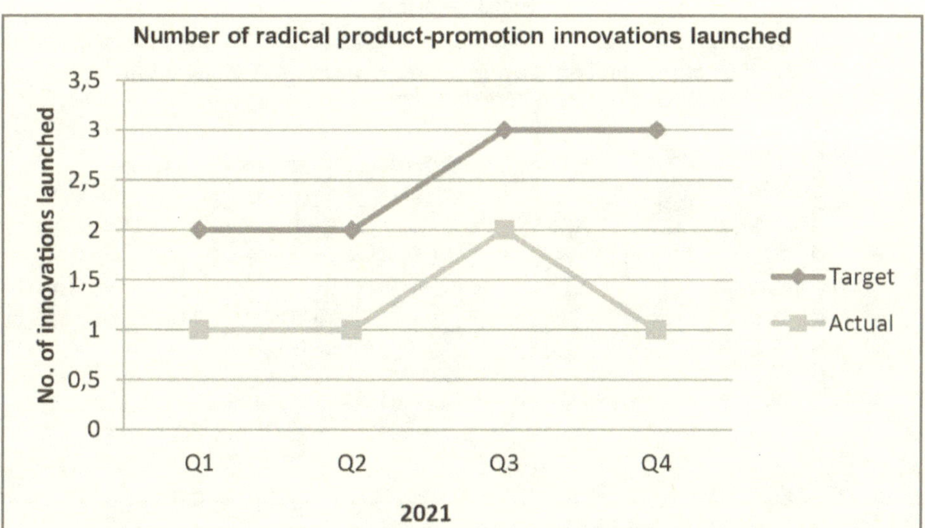

Figure 3-26

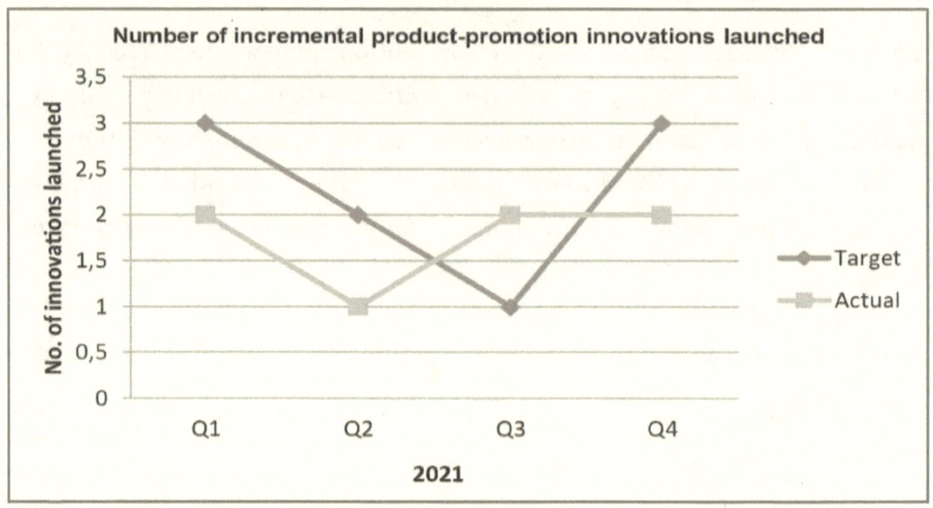

Figures 3-27 and 3-28 show the number of radical and incremental cost saving–focused product-promotion innovations (category 2) implemented in each quarter of 2021 (target and actual).

Figure 3-27

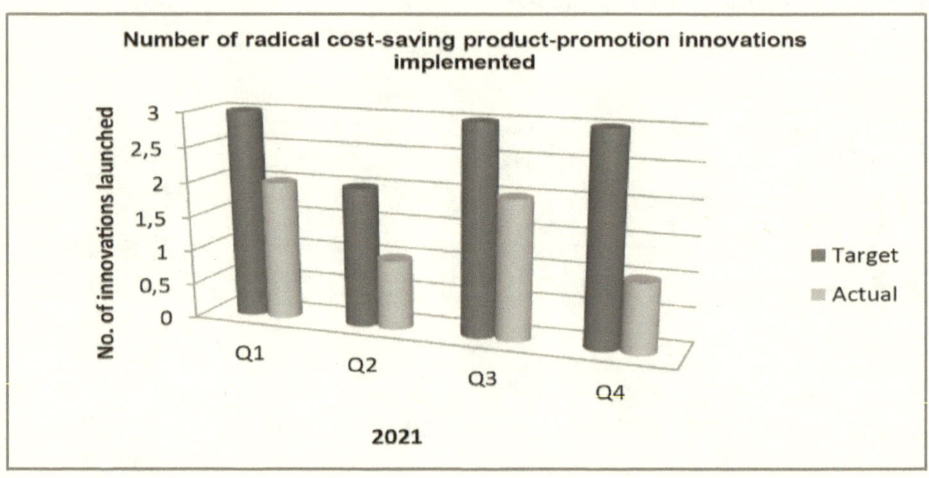

Figure 3-28

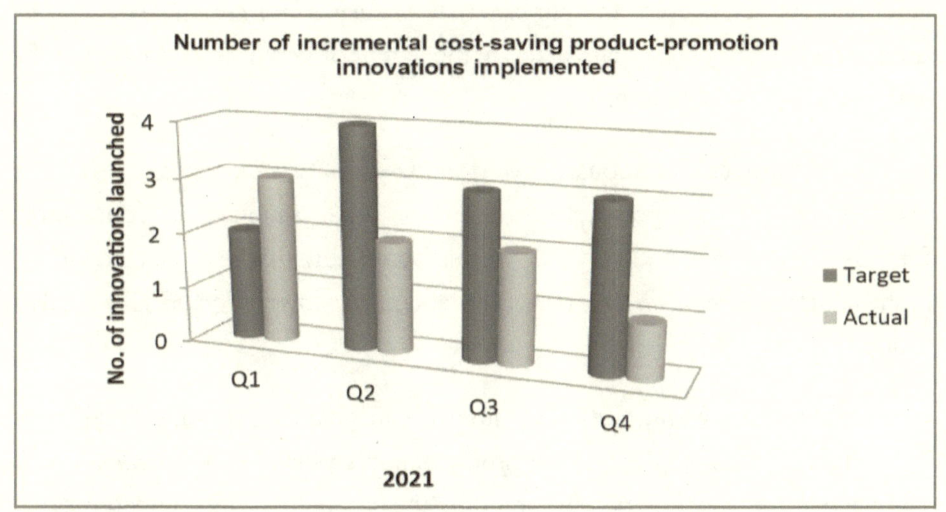

Similar charts (for revenue-generation or cost saving–focused innovations) would be created to present the number of radical and incremental marketing innovations implemented over a particular period in three of the other four units of the marketing department:

- Product-delivery unit
- Pricing unit
- Packaging unit

Absent from this list is the new-markets unit; because of the different format used for presenting the results of this unit, it is covered separately in the following subsection.

New-Markets Unit: How Is Innovation Characterized in the Context of New Markets?

Recall that earlier in Step Two noted that the context of interpreting or expressing the extent of the newness or novelty of an innovation for new markets is different from the contexts of other types of marketing innovations, such as innovations in pricing, product promotion, product delivery, and product packaging. Similarly, when it comes to presenting innovations about new markets discovered, the phrases *new unserved market* and *new-market segment* are again used to characterize the extent of newness or novelty of the new-market ideas generated.

As mentioned previously, *new-market innovation ideas* refers to discovering novel markets not served by the organization or its competitors for existing products and services. In this book, new markets are categorized in the contexts of *new unserved markets* and *new-market segments*, defined as follows:

- *New unserved markets*: This involves discovering customer audiences for the company's existing products and services in a *completely new geographical location* unserved by the company or its competitors.
- *New-market segments*: This involves discovering *new customer segments* for the company's *existing products and services* within an *already-served geographical location*. In other words, it involves the discovery of new-market segments in a larger geographical location already served by both the company and its competitors. This can be thought of as an "incremental" new-market discovery.

The two simple diagrams in figures 3-29 and 3-30 illustrate the context of new markets. Figure 3-29 illustrates a new unserved market in a new geographical area, whereas figure 3-30 illustrates a new-market segment in an already-served geographical area.

Figure 3-29. New Unserved Market in a Particular Geographical Location

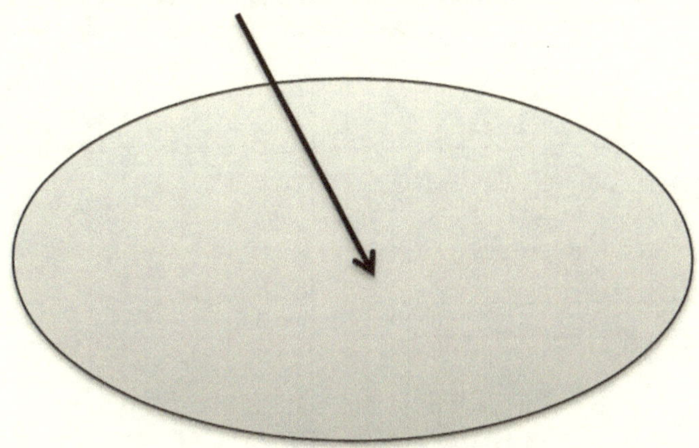

Figure 3-30. New-market segment in an already-served geographical location

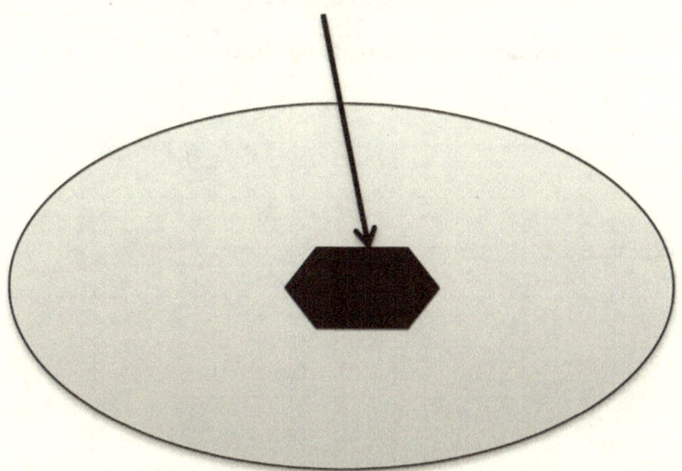

Presentation Format

The two simple charts in figures 3-31 and 3-32 show the number of new markets discovered in each of the two categories—new unserved markets (figure 3-31) and new-market segments (figure 3-32)—during the four quarters of 2021 (target and actual).

Figure 3-31

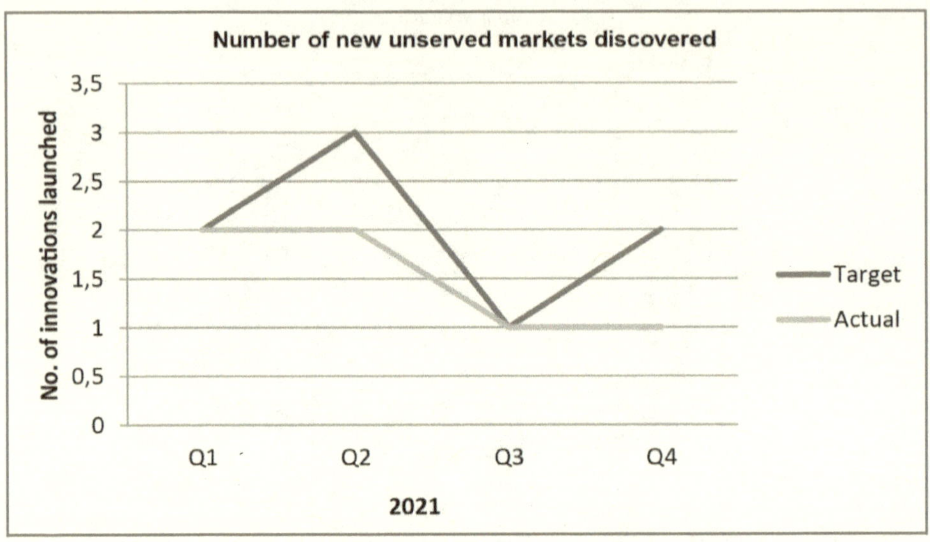

Figure 3-32

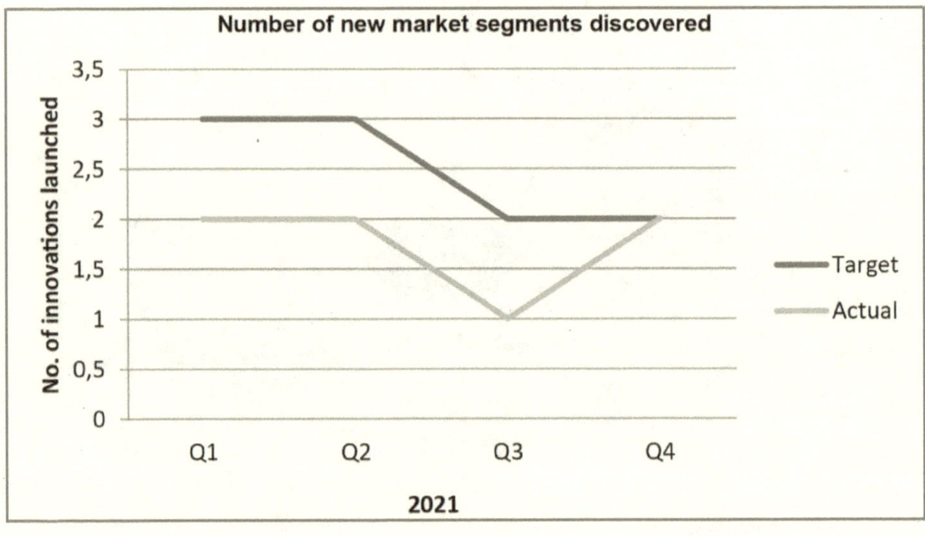

Customer Service Department

The last example of determining innovations launched or implemented by the core functional units of DM Personal Care Products is for the customer service department. The previous section on determining and presenting the number of customer service innovation ideas generated emphasized the importance of bearing in mind how the customer service components of an organization are structured for the purposes of innovation performance. The presentation of the customer service innovations launched or implemented is similar to the approach used earlier to present the number of customer service innovation ideas generated (see the discussion earlier in this chapter under "Innovation Output Measurement"). The presentation approach for customer service innovations launched or implemented is categorized as follows:

- Customer service innovations designed to support the delivery of product offerings *before* purchase
- Customer service innovations designed to support the delivery of product offerings *during* purchase
- Customer service innovations designed to support the delivery of product offerings *after* purchase
- Customer service innovations aimed at improving the quality of interaction between the company and its customers at all touchpoints

Presentation Format

Figures 3-33 and 3-34 show the number of *before-purchase* radical and incremental customer service innovations launched or implemented in each quarter of 2021 (target and actual).

Figure 3-33

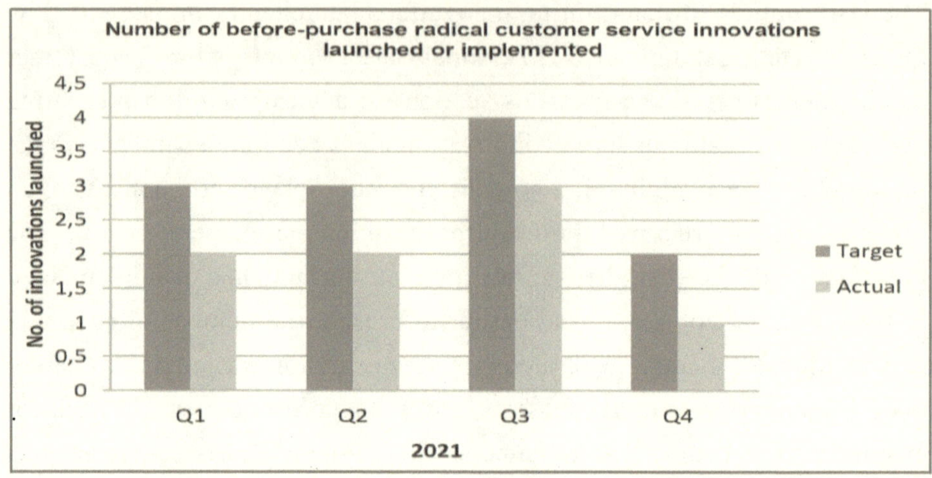

Figure 3-34

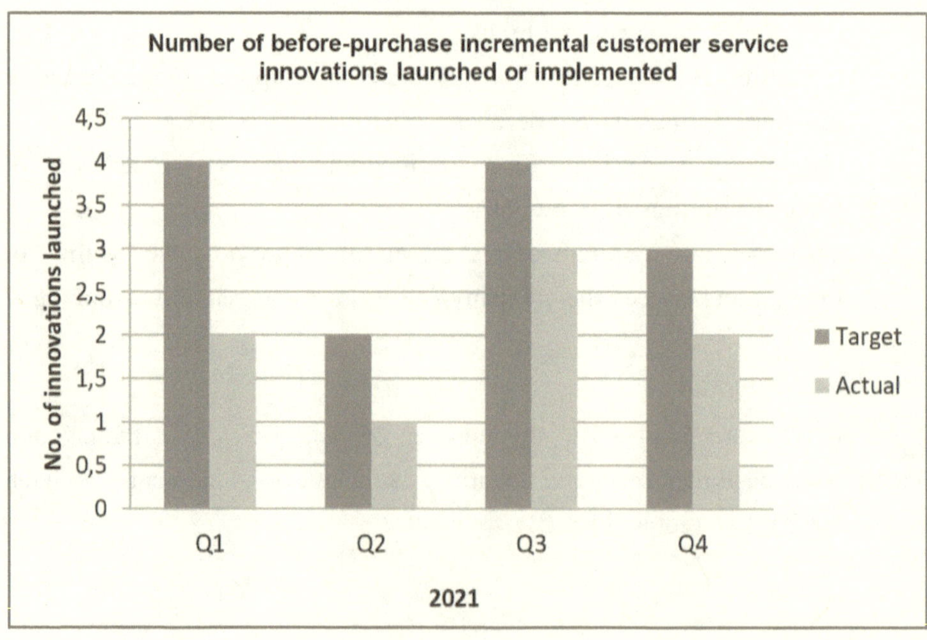

Similar charts would be created to present the number of radical and incremental customer service innovations implemented during the same period in each of the other three categories:

- *During-purchase* customer service innovations
- *After-purchase* customer service innovations
- *All-touch-points* customer service innovations

Presenting Radical and Incremental Innovations in Support Functional Units

The introduction chapter section of part III of this book noted that in addition to implementing innovation-support initiatives aimed at advancing the culture of innovation across the functional units of the organization, organizations need to generate innovative ideas for cost-saving and efficiency purposes in support functional units. Thus, this section illustrates how to present cost-saving innovations in the contexts of the five support functional units of DM Personal Care Products:

- Procurement department
- HR department
- Finance and accounting department
- IT department
- Corporate affairs department

Figures 3-35 and 3-36 show the number of radical and incremental IT cost-saving innovations implemented during the four quarters of 2021 (target and actual).

Figure 3-35

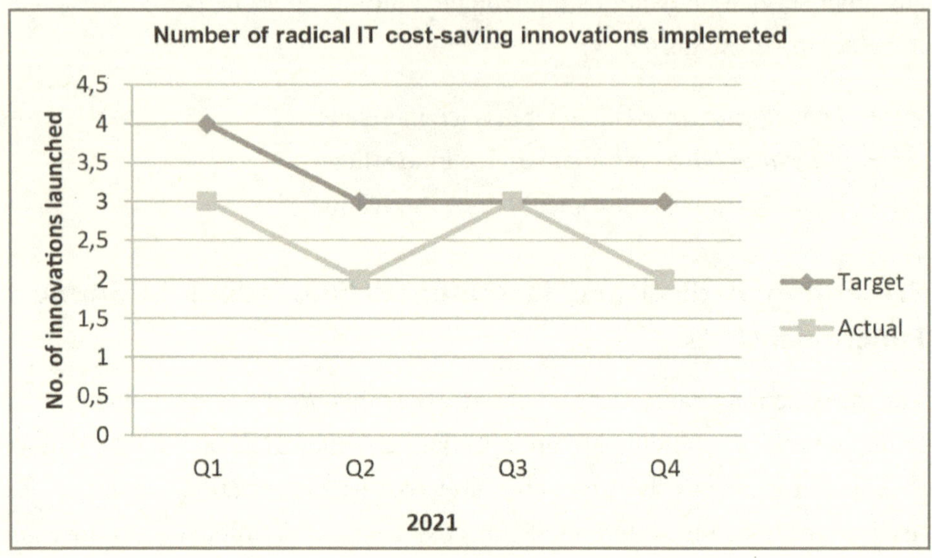

Figure 3-36

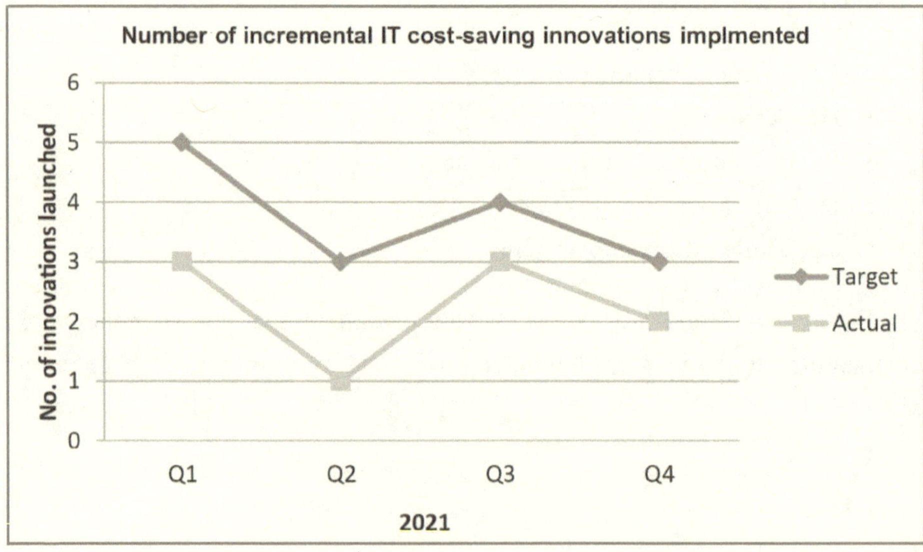

Similar charts would be created to present the number of radical and incremental cost-saving innovations implemented over the same period in each of the other four support functional units of DM Personal Care Products.

Innovation-Results Evaluation

As in the two earlier sections on innovation input measurement and innovation output measurement, the final part of this section provides an example of how to evaluate the innovation results presented in the previous subsections.

Once the number of innovations launched or implemented in both core and support functional units over a particular period has been presented, the next step is to assess whether the number of innovations launched or implemented during the period under review met the set goal or targets. Tables 3-13 through 3-15 provide examples of how the innovation-results evaluation can be applied to three of the functional units of DM Personal Care Products: the product-development unit (Table 3-13), marketing department (Table 3-14), and procurement department (Table 3-15).

Table 3-13. Example of Evaluating Innovation-Results

<table>
<tr><td colspan="5">Name of Department: Product-development unit

Date: April 30, 2021</td></tr>
<tr><td colspan="5">Purpose of Evaluation: To assess whether the goal of launching a particular number of radical and incremental product innovations in this category during the period under review (e.g., January–April of 2021) was achieved

The worksheet is divided into the four product segments of the product-development department of DM Personal Care Products, as follows:

• Part A: Body-lotions segment
• Part B: Skin-cleansing segment
• Part C: Hair-care segment
• Part D: Hand-washing segment</td></tr>
<tr><td colspan="5" align="center">Part A

Number of radical and incremental product innovations launched in the body-lotions segment</td></tr>
<tr><td colspan="5">Radical: Number of radical innovations launched during the period under review</td></tr>
<tr><td rowspan="2">Was the target for this product category achieved? (check "Yes" or "No")</td><td>Yes</td><td>Comment</td><td>No</td><td>Comment</td></tr>
<tr><td></td><td>If yes, indicate the percentage achieved.

Reasons: What factors are responsible for achieving or exceeding the set target?</td><td></td><td>If no, by what percentage was the target missed?

Reasons: What factors are responsible for not meeting the projected target?</td></tr>
</table>

table continues on next page

<table>
<tr><td colspan="5">Incremental: Number of incremental innovations launched during the period under review</td></tr>
<tr><td rowspan="2">Was the target for this product category achieved? (check “Yes” or “No”)</td><td>Yes</td><td>Comment</td><td>No</td><td>Comment</td></tr>
<tr><td></td><td>If yes, indicate the percentage achieved.
Reasons: What factors are responsible for achieving or exceeding the set target?</td><td></td><td>If no, by what percentage was the target missed?
Reasons: What factors are responsible for not meeting the projected target?</td></tr>
<tr><td colspan="5">Part B
Number of radical and incremental product innovations launched in the skin-cleansing segment</td></tr>
<tr><td colspan="5">Radical: Number of radical innovations launched during the period under review</td></tr>
<tr><td rowspan="2">Was the target for this product category achieved? (check “Yes” or “No”)</td><td>Yes</td><td>Comment</td><td>No</td><td>Comment</td></tr>
<tr><td></td><td>If yes, indicate the percentage achieved.
Reasons: What factors are responsible for achieving or exceeding the set target?</td><td></td><td>If no, by what percentage was the target missed?
Reasons: What factors are responsible for not meeting the projected target?</td></tr>
</table>

table continues on next page

<table>
<tr><td colspan="5">Incremental: Number of incremental innovations launched during the period under review</td></tr>
<tr><td rowspan="2">Was the target for this product category achieved? (check "Yes" or "No")</td><td>Yes</td><td>Comment</td><td>No</td><td>Comment</td></tr>
<tr><td></td><td>If yes, indicate the percentage achieved.
Reasons: What factors are responsible for achieving or exceeding the set target?</td><td></td><td>If no, by what percentage was the target missed?
Reasons: What factors are responsible for not meeting the projected target?</td></tr>
<tr><td colspan="5">Part C
Number of radical and incremental product innovations launched in the hair-care segment</td></tr>
<tr><td colspan="5">Radical: Number of radical innovations launched during the period under review</td></tr>
<tr><td rowspan="2">Was the target for this product category achieved? (check "Yes" or "No")</td><td>Yes</td><td>Comment</td><td>No</td><td>Comment</td></tr>
<tr><td></td><td>If yes, indicate the percentage achieved.
Reasons: What factors are responsible for achieving or exceeding the set target?</td><td></td><td>If no, by what percentage was the target missed?
Reasons: What factors are responsible for not meeting the projected target?</td></tr>
</table>

table continues on next page

Incremental: **Number of incremental innovations launched during the period under review**				
Was the target for this product category achieved? (check "Yes" or "No")	**Yes**	**Comment**	**No**	**Comment**
		If yes, indicate the percentage achieved. **Reasons:** *What factors are responsible for achieving or exceeding the set target?*		If no, by what percentage was the target missed? **Reasons:** *What factors are responsible for not meeting the projected target?*
Part D **Number of *radical* and *incremental* product innovations launched in the hand-washing segment**				
Radical: **Number of radical innovations launched during the period under review**				
Was the target for this product category achieved? (check "Yes" or "No")	**Yes**	**Comment**	**No**	**Comment**
		If yes, indicate the percentage achieved. **Reasons:** *What factors are responsible for achieving or exceeding the set target?*		If no, by what percentage was the target missed? **Reasons:** *What factors are responsible for not meeting the projected target?*

table continues on next page

Incremental: **Number of incremental innovations launched during the period under review**				
Was the target for this product category achieved? (check "Yes" or "No")	**Yes**	**Comment**	**No**	**Comment**
		If yes, indicate the percentage achieved. **Reasons:** *What factors are responsible for achieving or exceeding the set target?*		If no, by what percentage was the target missed? **Reasons:** *What factors are responsible for not meeting the projected target?*

Table 3-14. Example of Evaluating Marketing-Related Innovations

<table>
<tr><td colspan="5">Name of Department: Marketing department
Date: April 30, 2021</td></tr>
<tr><td colspan="5">Purpose of evaluation: To assess whether the goal of launching a particular number of radical and incremental marketing-related innovations during the period under review (e.g., January–April of 2021) was achieved
The worksheet is divided according to the subunits of the marketing department of DM Personal Care Products, as follows:
• Part A: Product delivery
• Part B: Pricing
• Part C: Product promotion
• Part D: New markets
• Part E: Packaging</td></tr>
<tr><td colspan="5">Part A
Product-delivery innovations</td></tr>
<tr><td colspan="5">Number of radical and incremental product-delivery innovations</td></tr>
<tr><td colspan="5">Radical: Number of radical product-delivery innovations launched or implemented during the period under review</td></tr>
<tr><td rowspan="2">Was the target for this category achieved? (check "Yes" or "No")</td><td>Yes</td><td>Comment</td><td>No</td><td>Comment</td></tr>
<tr><td></td><td>If yes, indicate the percentage achieved.
Reasons: What factors are responsible for achieving or exceeding the set target?</td><td></td><td>If no, by what percentage was the target missed?
Reasons: What factors are responsible for not meeting the projected target?</td></tr>
</table>

table continues on next page

Incremental: **Number of incremental product-delivery innovations launched or implemented during the period under review**				
Was the target for this category achieved? (check "Yes" or "No")	**Yes**	**Comment**	**No**	**Comment**
		If yes, indicate the percentage achieved. **Reasons:** *What factors are responsible for achieving or exceeding the set target?*		If no, by what percentage was the target missed? **Reasons:** *What factors are responsible for not meeting the projected target?*
Part B **Pricing innovations**				
Number of *radical* and *incremental* pricing innovations implemented for existing products during the period under review				
Radical: **Number of radical pricing innovations implemented for existing products during the period under review**				
Was the target for this category achieved? (check "Yes" or "No")	**Yes**	**Comment**	**No**	**Comment**
		If yes, indicate the percentage achieved. **Reasons:** *What factors are responsible for achieving or exceeding the set target?*		If no, by what percentage was the target missed? **Reasons:** *What factors are responsible for not meeting the projected target?*

table continues on next page

<table>
<tr><td colspan="5">Incremental: Number of incremental pricing innovations implemented for existing products during the period under review</td></tr>
<tr><td rowspan="2">Was the target for this category achieved? (check "Yes" or "No")</td><td>Yes</td><td>Comment</td><td>No</td><td>Comment</td></tr>
<tr><td></td><td>If yes, indicate the percentage achieved.
Reasons: What factors are responsible for achieving or exceeding the set target?</td><td></td><td>If no, by what percentage was the target missed?
Reasons: What factors are responsible for not meeting the projected target?</td></tr>
<tr><td colspan="5">Part C
Product-promotion innovations</td></tr>
<tr><td colspan="5">Number of radical and incremental product-promotion innovations implemented for existing products during the period under review</td></tr>
<tr><td colspan="5">Radical: Number of radical product-promotion innovations implemented for existing products during the period under review</td></tr>
<tr><td rowspan="2">Was the target for this category achieved? (check "Yes" or "No")</td><td>Yes</td><td>Comment</td><td>No</td><td>Comment</td></tr>
<tr><td></td><td>If yes, indicate the percentage achieved.
Reasons: What factors are responsible for achieving or exceeding the set target?</td><td></td><td>If no, by what percentage was the target missed?
Reasons: What factors are responsible for not meeting the projected target?</td></tr>
</table>

table continues on next page

<table>
<tr><td colspan="5">Incremental: Number of incremental product-promotion innovations implemented for existing products during the period under review</td></tr>
<tr><td rowspan="2">Was the target for this category achieved? (check “Yes” or “No”)</td><td>Yes</td><td>Comment</td><td>No</td><td>Comment</td></tr>
<tr><td></td><td>If yes, indicate the percentage achieved.
Reasons: What factors are responsible for achieving or exceeding the set target?</td><td></td><td>If no, by what percentage was the target missed?
Reasons: What factors are responsible for not meeting the projected target?</td></tr>
<tr><td colspan="5">Part D
New-markets innovations</td></tr>
<tr><td colspan="5">Number of new unserved markets discovered and number of new-market segments discovered during the period under review</td></tr>
<tr><td colspan="5">New unserved markets: Number of new unserved markets discovered for existing products (i.e., completely new geographical locations not served by the organization or its competitors) during the period under review</td></tr>
<tr><td rowspan="2">Was the target for this category achieved? (check “Yes” or “No”)</td><td>Yes</td><td>Comment</td><td>No</td><td>Comment</td></tr>
<tr><td></td><td>If yes, indicate the percentage achieved.
Reasons: What factors are responsible for achieving or exceeding the set target?</td><td></td><td>If no, by what percentage was the target missed?
Reasons: What factors are responsible for not meeting the projected target?</td></tr>
</table>

table continues on next page

<table>
<tr><td colspan="5">New-market segments: Number of new-market segments discovered during the period under review for existing products within existing market or geographical locations</td></tr>
<tr><td rowspan="2">Was the target for this category achieved? (check “Yes” or “No”)</td><td>Yes</td><td>Comment</td><td>No</td><td>Comment</td></tr>
<tr><td></td><td>If yes, indicate the percentage achieved.
Reasons: What factors are responsible for achieving or exceeding the set target?</td><td></td><td>If no, by what percentage was the target missed?
Reasons: What factors are responsible for not meeting the projected target?</td></tr>
<tr><td colspan="5">Part E
Packaging innovations</td></tr>
<tr><td colspan="5">Number of radical and incremental packaging innovations launched during the period under review</td></tr>
<tr><td colspan="5">Radical: Number of radical packaging innovations launched during the period under review</td></tr>
<tr><td rowspan="2">Was the target for this category achieved? (check “Yes” or “No”)</td><td>Yes</td><td>Comment</td><td>No</td><td>Comment</td></tr>
<tr><td></td><td>If yes, indicate the percentage achieved.
Reasons: What factors are responsible for achieving or exceeding the set target?</td><td></td><td>If no, by what percentage was the target missed?
Reasons: What factors are responsible for not meeting the projected target?</td></tr>
</table>

table continues on next page

Incremental: **Number of incremental packaging innovations launched during the period under review**				
Was the target for this category achieved? (check "Yes" or "No")	**Yes**	**Comment**	**No**	**Comment**
		If yes, indicate the percentage achieved. **Reasons:** *What factors are responsible for achieving or exceeding the set target?*		If no, by what percentage was the target missed? **Reasons:** *What factors are responsible for not meeting the projected target?*

A similar approach to that shown in Tables 3-13 and 3-14 would be applied to the other core functional units of DM Personal Care Products:

- Manufacturing-processes department
- Customer service department

Table 3-15 shows how the innovation-results evaluation worksheet can be applied to the support functional units of DM Personal Care Products, using the procurement department as an example.

Table 3-15. Example of Evaluating Cost-Saving Procurement Innovations

<table>
<tr><td colspan="5">Name of Department: Procurement department

Date: April 30, 2021</td></tr>
<tr><td colspan="5">Purpose of evaluation: To assess whether the goal of implementing a particular number of radical and incremental cost-saving procurement innovations during the period under review (e.g., January–April of 2021) was achieved

The worksheet is divided into two parts, as follows:<ul><li>Part A: Number of radical cost-saving procurement innovations implemented during the period under review</li><li>Part B: Number of incremental cost-saving procurement innovations implemented during the period under review</li></ul></td></tr>
<tr><td colspan="5">Part A

Number of radical cost-saving procurement innovations implemented during the period under review</td></tr>
<tr><td rowspan="2">Was the target for this category achieved? (check "Yes" or "No")</td><td>Yes</td><td>Comment</td><td>No</td><td>Comment</td></tr>
<tr><td></td><td>If yes, indicate the percentage achieved.

Reasons: What factors are responsible for achieving or exceeding the set target?</td><td></td><td>If no, by what percentage was the target missed?

Reasons: What factors are responsible for not meeting the projected target?</td></tr>
</table>

table continues on next page

Part B **Number of incremental cost-saving procurement innovations implemented during the period under review**				
Was the target for this category achieved? (check "Yes" or "No")	**Yes**	**Comment**	**No**	**Comment**
		If yes, indicate the percentage achieved. **Reasons:** *What factors are responsible for achieving or exceeding the set target?*		If no, by what percentage was the target missed? **Reasons:** *What factors are responsible for not meeting the projected target?*

Similar evaluation worksheets would be created to show the number of radical and incremental innovations implemented over the same period in each of the other four support functional units of DM Personal Care Products:

- HR department
- Finance and accounting department
- IT department
- Corporate affairs department

Step Four

INNOVATION IMPACT MEASUREMENT

Overview

We've now covered three metrics of measuring innovation performance: innovation input measurement, innovation output measurement, and innovation results measurement. The fourth, and last, metric is *innovation impact measurement*.

The Introduction section of this book defines *innovation* as a process that involves identifying a problem or need, generating a new idea that has not been seen on the market before, turning the idea into a solution to address the identified need, and then converting the solution into monetary value. The end result of any innovation performance activity is the commercial or monetary value gained; this section provides a mechanism to determine that. Step Four covers (1) definitions, (2) metrics for determining innovation impact, (3) illustration of how to determine innovation impact measurement, and (4) innovation impact evaluation.

Definitions

To understand innovation impact measurement, it is necessary to first interpret the context of the phrase *innovation impact.*

Definition of *Innovation Impact*

Let's begin by defining the word *impact.* According to the *Merriam-Webster* online dictionary, the word *impact* means "to have an effect" on something. In the context of innovation, *innovation impact* can be defined as an innovation-performance metric that captures the monetary effect of an innovation on the organization.

Definition of *Innovation Impact Measurement*

Innovation impact measurement can be defined as a dimension of innovation-performance measurement that involves determining the effect of an innovation on the organization's commercial and monetary value in terms of revenue, cost savings, and other aspects, such as market share, stock price, and market value.

Data Compilation and Collaboration

The introduction section of this book noted that leading and managing innovation across functional units involves a combination of various innovation-oriented initiatives and activities across these units. In other words, in order to make innovation a permanent habit across the organization, every functional unit has to play a role. That said, compiling and reporting data on innovation impact is one of the vital aspects of innovation-performance measurement because it is the final determination of the return on investment in innovation initiatives and activities. The question is, *whose role is it to compile data on innovation impact?* Generally, because finance and accounting teams are traditionally responsible for reporting the financial matters of an organization, it should be their responsibility to determine the content and appropriate reporting format and style for presenting data on various aspects of innovation impact. In terms of collaboration, just as finance teams collaborate or confer with other functional units when creating content for conventional corporate financial reporting, finance teams should collaborate and confer closely with other functional units when putting together content on innovation impact.

Innovation-Life Time Frame

The first factor to take into account when determining innovation impact is the innovation-life time frame.

What does *innovation-life time frame* mean? It is a period set by an organization within which an innovation will qualify to be called or characterized as an innovation and after which it will cease to be called or characterized as an innovation.

The innovation-life time frame is vital when it comes to assessing and reporting the innovation impact on monetary value because only innovations that have not elapsed should be included in innovation-performance reports.

Thus, one of the initial tasks to undertake when adopting a framework for innovation-performance reporting is to define the period within which an innovation will carry the *innovation* tag. This would be done by enacting a policy stating the expiration time frame in terms of when an innovation will cease to be referred to as an innovation. Once the period elapses, the innovation—whether a product innovation, process innovation, marketing innovation, or so forth—will no longer carry the *innovation* tag and will be referred to using the same terminology as that used for other existing product offerings, process components, marketing components, customer service components or support functional components. Regarding whether there's a standard time frame in which innovations should carry the *innovation* tag, the time frame varies from company to company depending on the innovation-performance framework of the organization. Thus, the company has to clearly define the innovation-life time period, which should be communicated to all the workforces across functional units. For instance, "Any type and degree of innovation shall be referred to as an innovation for no more than three years.

Meaning that after three years, such a product, process, marketing component, or any other type of innovation shall no longer carry the *innovation* tag or be referred to as an innovation." Additionally, the leadership could regularly publicize across the organization innovations that the company has "in stock" as well as those that are due to expire.

Metrics for Determining Innovation Impact

How do you determine innovation impact? The following are suggested examples of metrics that can be used to determine the monetary value created by innovations launched or implemented during the period under review:

- Percentages of revenue generated from new products or services during the period under review
- Percentages of revenue from marketing innovations, including the following:
    - Percentages of revenue generated from pricing innovations for existing products and services
    - Percentages of revenue generated or savings gained from promotion innovations for existing products or services
    - Percentages of revenue generated or savings gained from packaging innovations for existing products
- Percentages of revenue from new markets, including the following:
    - Percentages of revenue generated from existing products or services in new unserved markets in geographical locations not served by either the organization or its competitors
    - Percentages of revenue generated from existing products or services in new-market segments within existing markets or geographical locations
- Amount of savings gained as a result of cost-saving innovations implemented across functional units of the organization during the period under review

Illustration:
How to Determine Innovation Impact Measurement

Let's return to the functional units of DM Personal Care Products, our fictitious example company, to illustrate how to present revenues generated from radical and incremental innovations launched and cost savings gained from radical and incremental cost-saving innovations implemented across functional units during the period under review. As in the previous sections on measuring innovation performance, the first step is to outline the core and support functional units of DM Personal Care Products:

Core functional units

- Product-development unit, with the following segments:
    - Body-lotions segment
    - Skin-cleansing segment
    - Hair-care segment
    - Hand-washing segment
- Manufacturing-processes department, (as mentioned earlier, the manufacturing-processes department comprises the same segments as the product-development unit).
- Marketing department, with the following units:
    - Pricing
    - Product promotion
    - Product delivery
    - New markets
    - Packaging
- Customer service department

Support functional units

- Procurement department
- HR department
- Finance and accounting department

- IT department
- Corporate affairs department

The second step is to show, by use of simple charts, the revenues generated from radical and incremental innovations launched and the cost savings gained from radical and incremental cost-saving innovations implemented. We begin with the product-development department.

Product-Development Department

The charts in figures 4-37 and 4-38 show revenues generated from radical and incremental innovations launched in a particular period in all the product segments:

- Body-lotions segment
- Skin-cleansing segment
- Hair-care segment
- Hand-washing segment

Radical body-lotion innovations: Assuming we wish to determine the amount of revenue (by percentage) generated by four *radical body-lotion innovations* launched between January and December of 2021, the simple steps are as follows:

- First, establish the number (in this case, four) and names of the radical body-lotion innovations launched during the period under review.
- Second, establish the amount generated by each of the four radical body-lotion innovations launched during the period under review.
- Third, establish the total amount of revenue generated by all four radical body-lotion innovations during the period under review.
- Fourth, present data showing the percentage of revenue generated by each of the radical body-lotion innovations launched during the period under review.

The two simple pie charts in figures 4-37 and 4-38 show the percentages of revenue generated from radical and incremental body-lotion innovations launched between January and December of 2021.

Figure 4-37 shows the percentage of revenue generated from each of the four radical body-lotion innovations launched between January and December of 2021.

For illustration purposes, the four radical body-lotion innovations launched are named as follows:

- Radical body-lotion innovation 1
- Radical body-lotion innovation 2
- Radical body-lotion innovation 3
- Radical body-lotion innovation 4

Figure 4-37

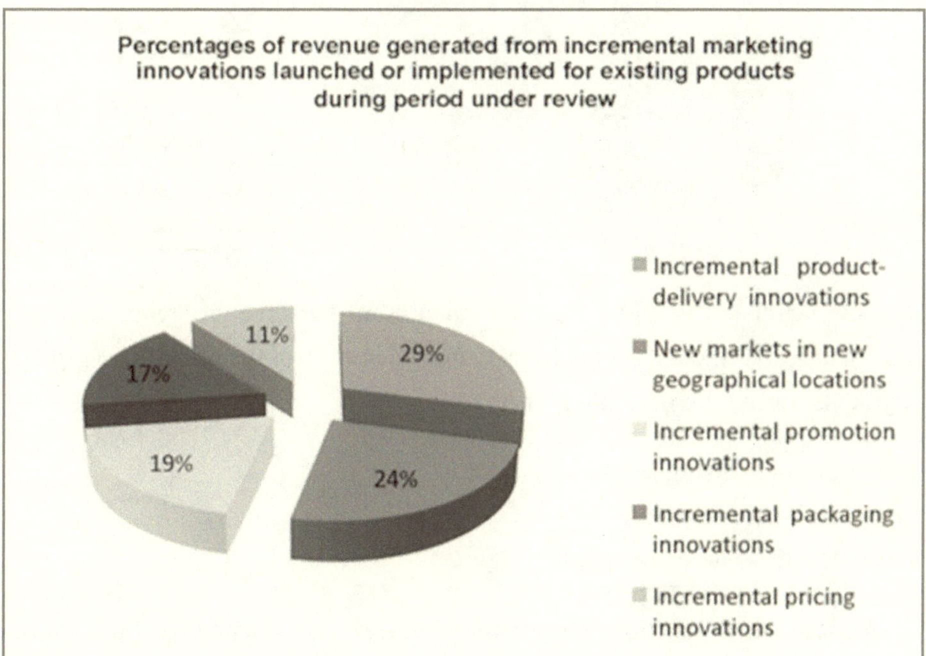

Similarly, figure 4-38 shows the percentages of revenue generated by the five incremental body-lotion innovations launched between January and December of 2021:

- Incremental body-lotion innovation 1
- Incremental body-lotion innovation 2
- Incremental body-lotion innovation 3
- Incremental body-lotion innovation 4
- Incremental body-lotion innovation 5

Figure 4-38

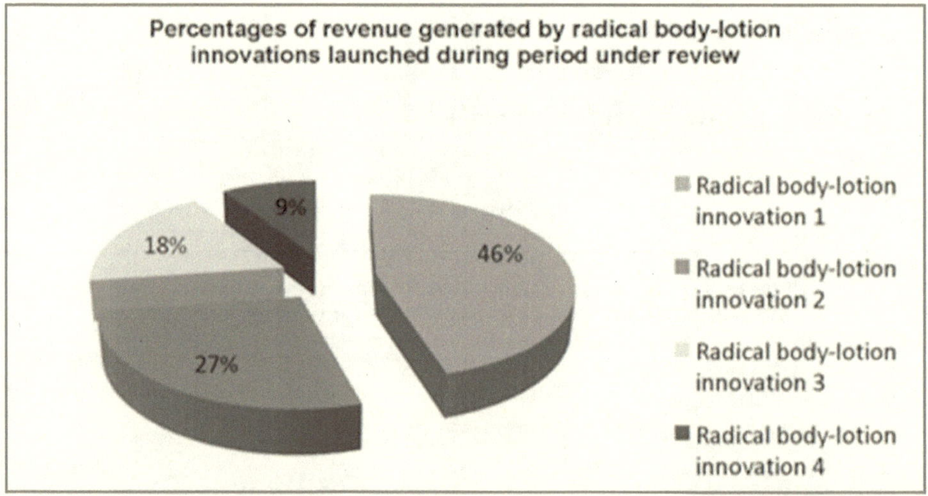

Similar charts would be created to present the revenue generated from radical and incremental innovations launched in each of the other three product segments during the period under review:

- Skin-cleansing segment
- Hair-care segment
- Hand-washing segment

As stated in the section on presenting innovations launched (i.e., innovation-results measurement), in cases where a product category has a number of product segments, for instance, if the skin-cleansing product segment had four product categories, the revenue generated from the radical and incremental innovations launched would be presented accordingly in each of the four product categories.

Manufacturing-Processes Department

The next example is for the manufacturing-processes department. Recall that this functional unit of DM Personal Care Products has the following manufacturing-processes categories:

- Body-lotions manufacturing-processes category
- Skin-cleansing manufacturing-processes category
- Hair-care manufacturing-processes category
- Hand-washing manufacturing-processes category

Assuming we wish to determine the amount of savings gained (by percentage) from manufacturing-processes innovations implemented between January and December of 2021, the simple steps are as follows:

- First, establish the number and names of all radical and incremental manufacturing-processes innovations implemented during the period under review.
- Second, establish the amount saved from each of the radical and incremental manufacturing-processes innovations implemented during the period under review.
- Third, establish the total amount of savings gained from the radical and incremental manufacturing-processes innovations during the period under review.
- Fourth, present data showing the percentage of savings gained from each of the radical and incremental manufacturing-processes innovations implemented during the period under review.

Assume we have savings gained from radical and incremental manufacturing-processes innovations implemented in the following four manufacturing-processes categories:

- Body-lotions manufacturing-processes innovations
- Skin-cleansing manufacturing-processes innovations

- Hair-care manufacturing-processes innovations
- Hand-washing manufacturing-processes innovations

The percentages of cost savings from these radical and incremental manufacturing innovations would be presented as shown in figure 4-39 for cost savings from radical manufacturing-processes innovations and figure 4-40 for cost savings from incremental manufacturing-processes innovations implemented in 2021.

Figure 4-39

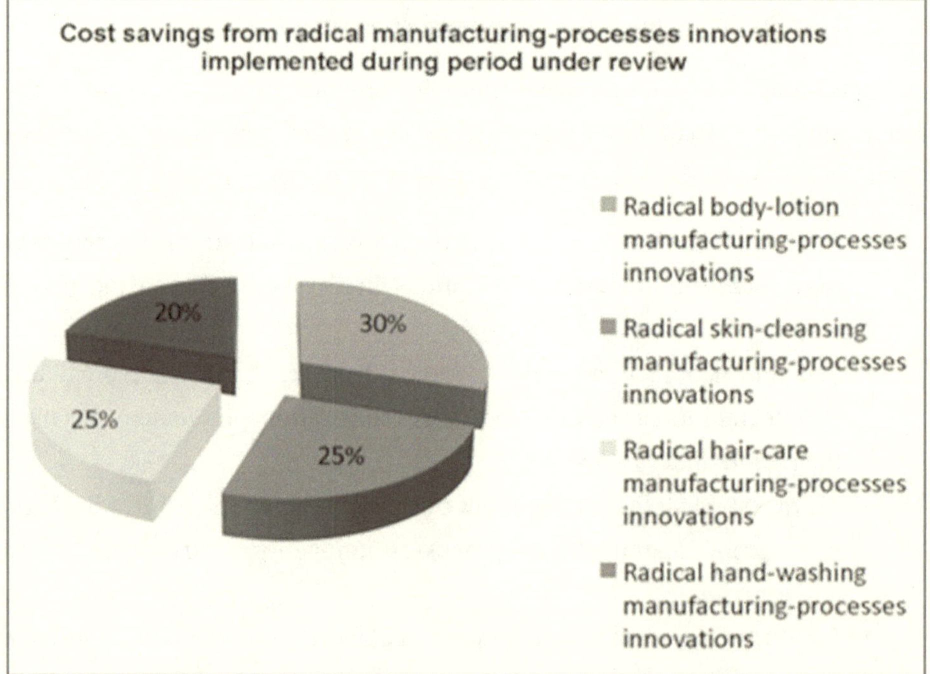

Figure 4-40

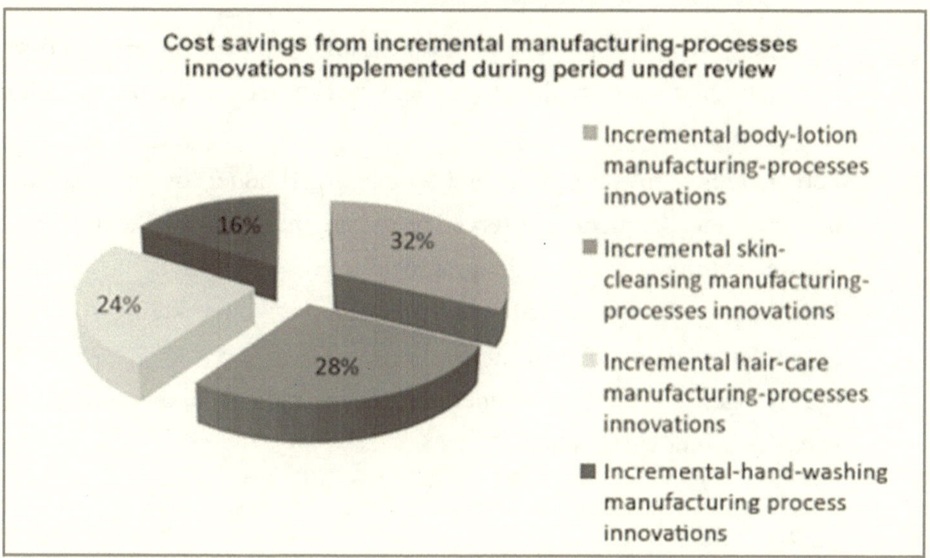

Marketing Department

Recall that marketing innovations are types of innovation developed and implemented in various segments of the marketing department and that the type of marketing innovation ideas generated will usually depend on how the organization characterizes or defines the segments that make up the marketing functional unit of the organization. That being said, this section illustrates how to present the monetary impact of marketing innovations based on the marketing functional units of DM Personal Care Products. In this illustration, the monetary impact is segmented into two categories: *revenues generated* and *cost savings*. The contexts of the two categories are outlined as follows:

Revenues Generated

- Percentages of revenue generated from radical and incremental innovative methods of delivering products to customers
- Percentages of revenue generated from pricing innovations for existing products and services

- Percentages of revenue generated from promotion innovations for existing products or services
- Percentages of revenue generated for existing products or services from new markets in geographical locations not served by the organization or its competitors
- Percentages of revenue generated for existing products or services from new customer segments not served by the organization or its competitors within existing markets or geographical locations
- Percentages of revenue generated from innovative marketing alliances to deliver products to customers
- Percentages of revenue generated from radical and incremental packaging innovations launched

Cost Savings

- Percentages of cost savings gained from radical and incremental innovative methods of delivering products to customers for existing products
- Percentages of cost savings gained from radical and incremental promotion innovations for existing products or services
- Percentages of cost savings gained from radical and incremental packaging innovations launched for existing products

Illustration

Assuming we want to determine the amount of revenue generated and cost savings gained (in percentage terms) from radical and incremental marketing innovations launched or implemented between January and December of 2018, the simple steps are as follows:

- First, establish the number and names of all radical and incremental marketing innovations launched or implemented during the period under review.

- Second, establish the amount of revenue generated or cost savings gained from each of the radical and incremental marketing innovations launched or implemented during the period under review.
- Third, establish the total amount of revenue generated and cost savings gained from radical and incremental marketing innovations during the period under review.
- Fourth, present data showing the percentages of revenue generated and cost savings gained from each of the radical and incremental marketing strategy innovations launched or implemented during the period under review.

Let's assume we're determining revenues generated and savings made from the following radical and incremental marketing innovations:

- Radical and incremental product-delivery innovations
- New unserved markets (i.e., completely new markets and new-market segments for existing products)
- Radical and incremental promotion innovations for existing products
- Radical and incremental pricing innovations for existing products
- Radical and incremental packaging innovations for existing products

The following subsections illustrate how to present this information.

Revenues Generated

The percentages of revenue generated from radical and incremental marketing innovations listed previously are presented in two pie charts: figure 4-41 is for the percentages of revenue generated from various radical marketing innovations launched or implemented for existing products in 2021, and figure 4-42 is for the percentages of revenue generated from various incremental marketing innovations launched or implemented for existing products in 2021.

Figure 4-41

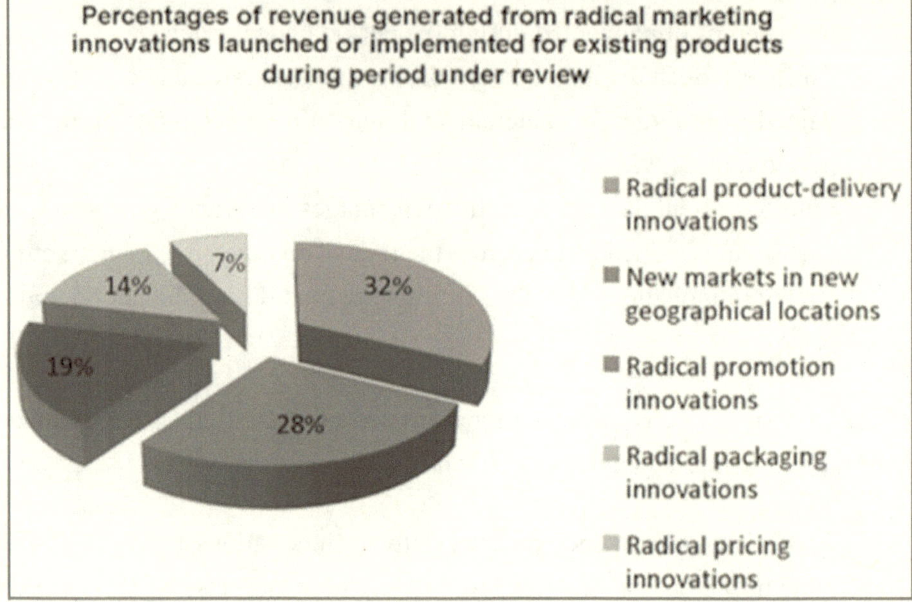

Figure 4-42

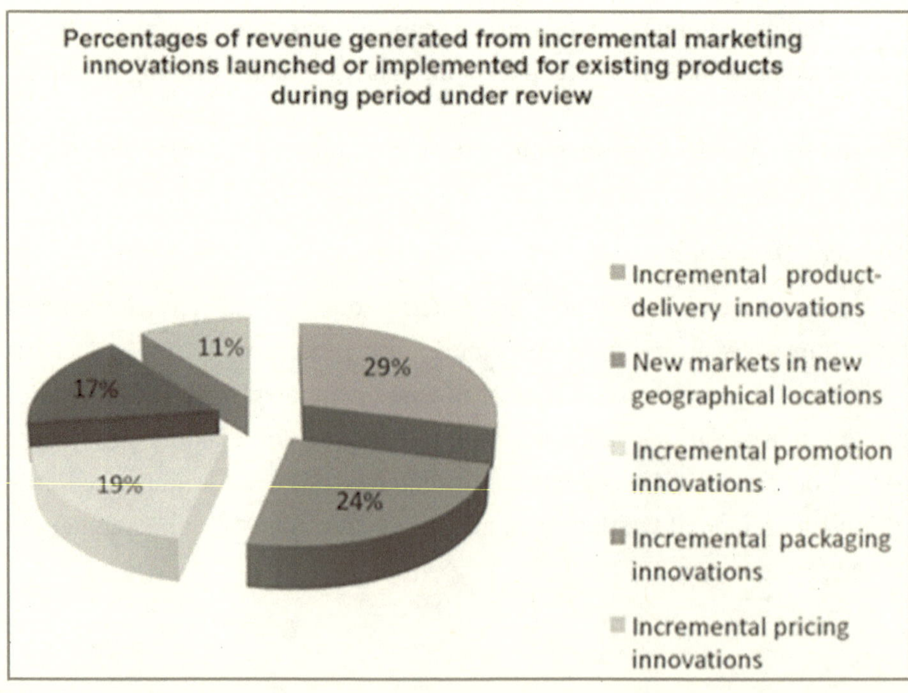

Cost Savings

Similarly, savings gained from radical and incremental cost-saving marketing innovations during the period under review are presented in two pie charts: figure 4-43 is for the percentages of cost savings gained from radical marketing innovations launched or implemented for existing products in 2021, and figure 4-44 is for the percentages of cost savings gained from incremental marketing innovations launched or implemented for existing products in 2021.

Figure 4-43

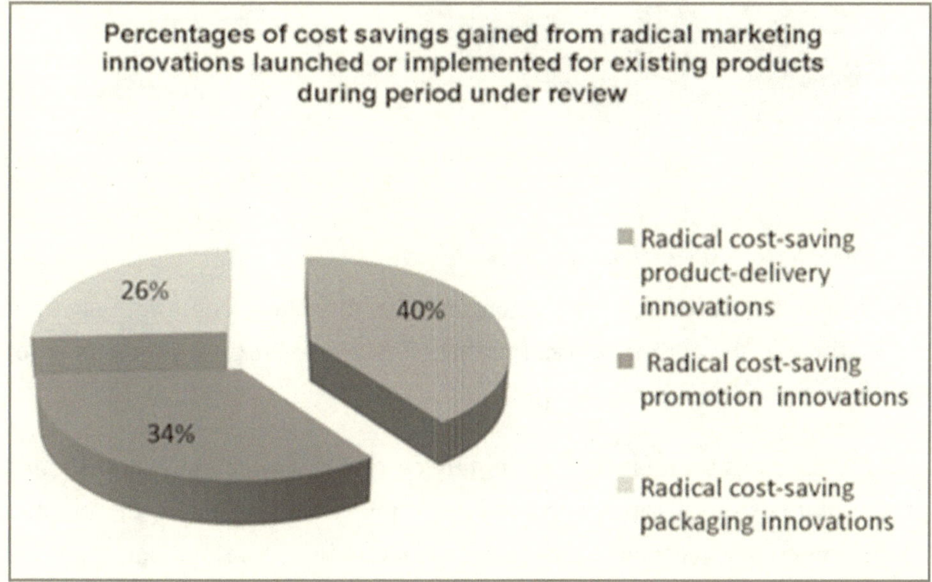

Figure 4-44

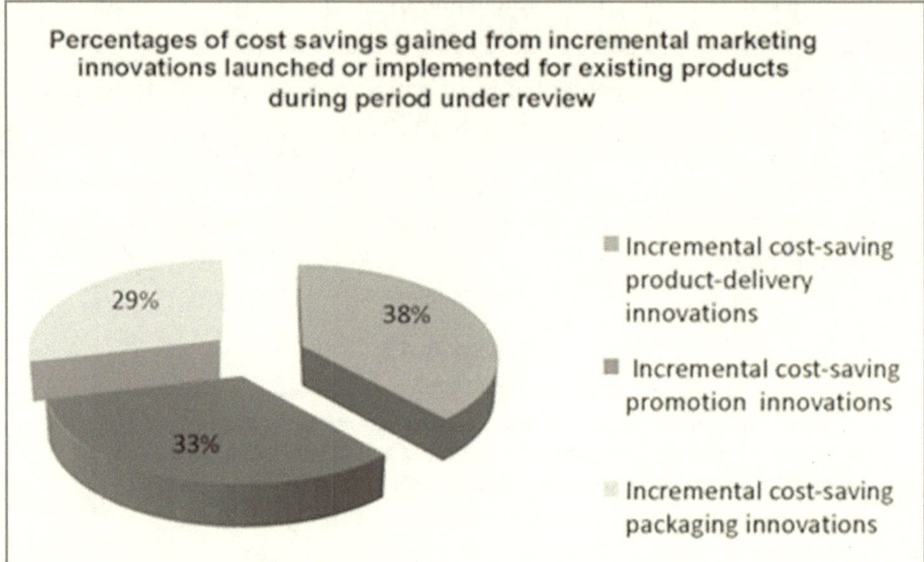

Customer Service Department

The last example on how to determine the monetary contributions from innovations in the core functional units of DM Personal Care Products is for the customer service department.

The previous sections on determining customer service innovations—that is, the number of customer service innovation ideas generated, the number of customer service innovation ideas undergoing development, and the number of customer service innovations launched—outlined the importance of understanding perspectives on customer service and how its functional components are structured. Similarly, when presenting the monetary contributions from customer service innovations launched or implemented, it's important to bear in mind how the customer service components of an organization are configured so that the presentation format for the monetary contributions generated from customer service innovations can be aligned with the configuration of the customer service components.

Illustration

There are two important aspects to bear in mind when determining and presenting the monetary contributions generated from customer service innovations, as follows:

- *Types of customer service innovations:* As stated previously, there are four types of customer service innovations:
    - Customer service innovations designed to support the delivery of product offerings *before* purchase
    - Customer service innovations designed to support the delivery of product offerings *during* purchase
    - Customer service innovations designed to support the delivery of product offerings *after* purchase
    - Customer service innovations aimed at improving the quality of interactions between the company and its customers at all touchpoints
- *Contexts of the monetary value generated:* The second important aspect to bear in mind when determining the monetary value generated from radical and incremental customer service innovations is that there are two contexts for the monetary value generated, as follows:
    - Revenue generated from various radical and incremental customer service innovations launched or implemented
    - Cost savings gained from various radical and incremental customer service innovations launched or implemented

Note that whatever format is used, these two contexts should be presented clearly in a manner that can be understood by all workforces.

Presentation Format

Assume we'd like to determine and present the amount of revenue generated and cost savings gained (in percentage terms) from before-purchase radical and incremental customer service innovations launched or implemented between January and December of 2021. The steps are as follows:

- First, establish the number and names of all radical and incremental before-purchase customer service innovations launched or implemented during the period under review
- Second, establish the amount of revenue generated and cost savings gained from each of the before-purchase radical and incremental customer service innovations launched or implemented during the period under review
- Third, establish the total amount of revenue generated and savings made from all before-purchase radical and incremental customer service innovations during the period under review
- Fourth, present data showing the percentage of revenue generated and savings gained from each of the before-purchase radical and incremental customer service innovations during the period under review

The next step is determining revenue generated and cost savings gained during the period under review, which have the following components:

Revenue Generated

- Revenue generated from four before-purchase radical customer service innovations launched or implemented during the period under review
- Revenue generated from four before-purchase incremental customer service innovations launched or implemented during the period under review

Cost Savings Gained

- Cost savings gained from four before-purchase radical customer service innovations during the period under review
- Cost savings gained from four before-purchase incremental customer service innovations during the period under review

Based on these categories of monetary value generated, the presentation will be divided into two categories: category 1 for revenue generation–focused customer service innovations and category 2 for cost savings–focused customer service innovations. For each of the two categories, follow these two steps:

- First, outline all before-purchase radical and incremental customer service innovations launched or implemented in each particular category during the period under review.
- Second, use pie charts to illustrate the monetary value generated by each innovation in both categories (i.e., categories 1 and 2).

For illustration purposes, the radical and incremental revenue generation–centered customer service innovations launched during the period under review (category 1) are identified by the numbers 1–4 for each set (radical and incremental), resulting in the following outline for the first step:

Radical customer service innovations launched or implemented:

- Before-purchase radical customer service innovation 1
- Before-purchase radical customer service innovation 2
- Before-purchase radical customer service innovation 3
- Before-purchase radical customer service innovation 4

Incremental customer service innovations launched or implemented:

- Before-purchase incremental customer service innovation 1
- Before-purchase incremental customer service innovation 2
- Before-purchase incremental customer service innovation 3
- Before-purchase incremental customer service innovation 4

Pie Chart Presentation of Revenue Generated

The percentages of revenue generated from the radical and incremental customer service innovations just listed are presented in two pie charts: figure 4-45 is for the percentages of revenue generated from before-purchase radical customer service innovations launched or implemented during the period under review, and figure 4-46 is for the percentages of revenue generated from before-purchase incremental customer service innovations launched or implemented during the period under review.

Figure 4-45

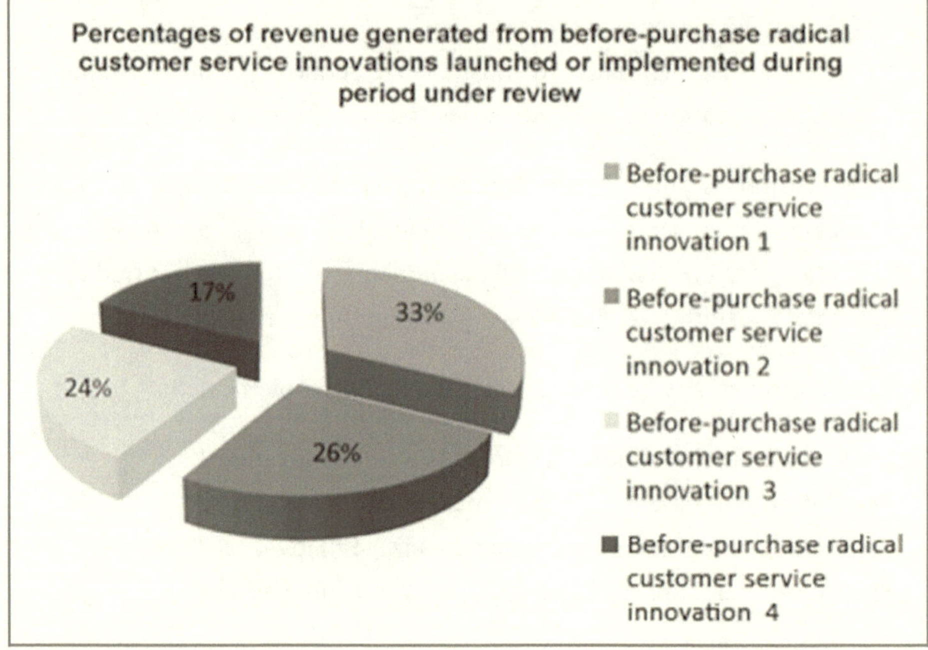

Figure 4-46

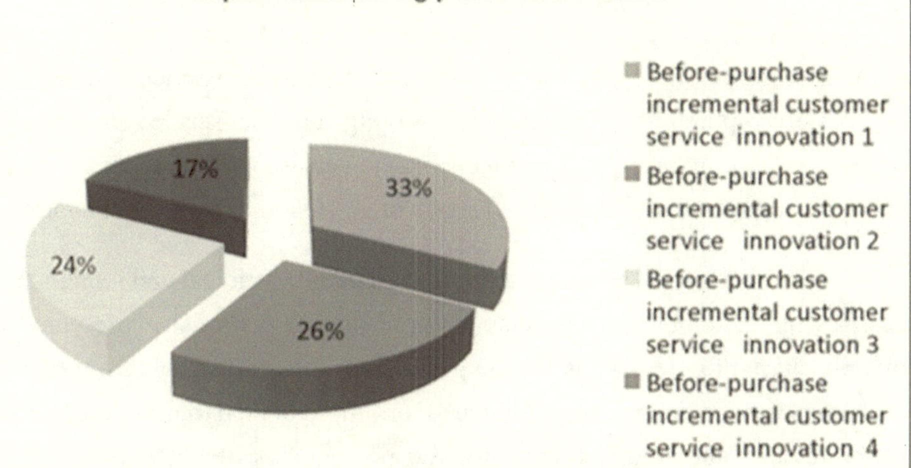

Pie Chart Presentation of Cost Savings Gained

Assuming there are four radical cost-saving customer service innovations and four incremental cost-saving customer service innovations launched or implemented during the period under review, as in the preceding section, the steps are as follows:

- The first step is to outline radical and incremental cost-saving customer service innovations launched or implemented during the period under review. (For illustration purposes, these are labeled using the numbers 1–4 for each set.)
- The second step is presentation of the data by use of pie charts.

The first step results in the following outline:

Radical cost-saving customer service innovations launched or implemented:

- Before-purchase radical cost-saving customer service innovation 1
- Before-purchase radical cost-saving customer service innovation 2

- Before-purchase radical cost-saving customer service innovation 3
- Before-purchase radical cost-saving customer service innovation 4

Incremental cost-saving customer service innovations launched or implemented:

- Before-purchase incremental cost-saving customer service innovation 1
- Before-purchase incremental cost-saving customer service innovation 2
- Before-purchase incremental cost-saving customer service innovation 3
- Before-purchase incremental cost-saving customer service innovation 4

The percentage of savings gained from each of the radical and incremental cost-saving customer service innovations in the previous list is presented in two pie charts: figure 4-47 is for the percentages of cost savings from radical customer service innovations launched or implemented during the period under review, and figure 4-48 is for the percentages of cost savings from incremental customer service innovations launched or implemented during the period under review.

Figure 4-47

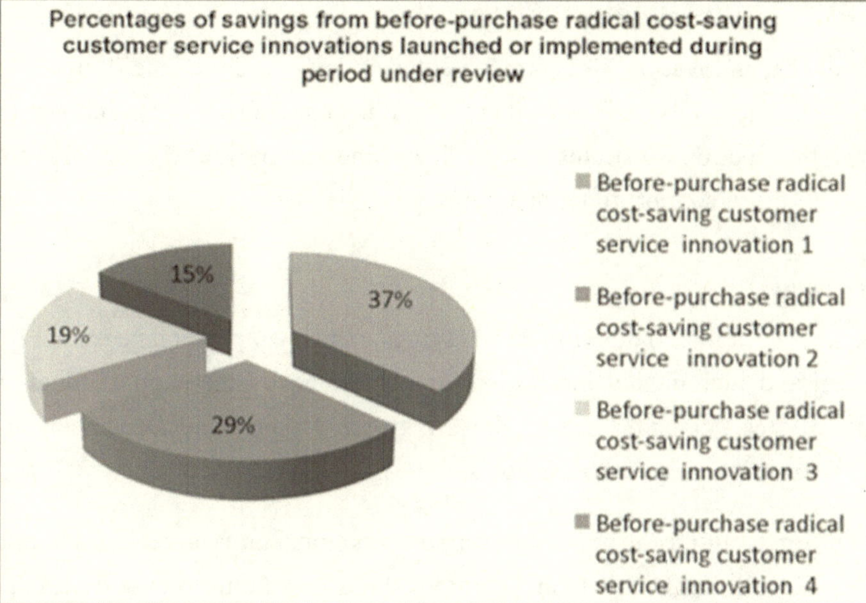

Figure 4-48

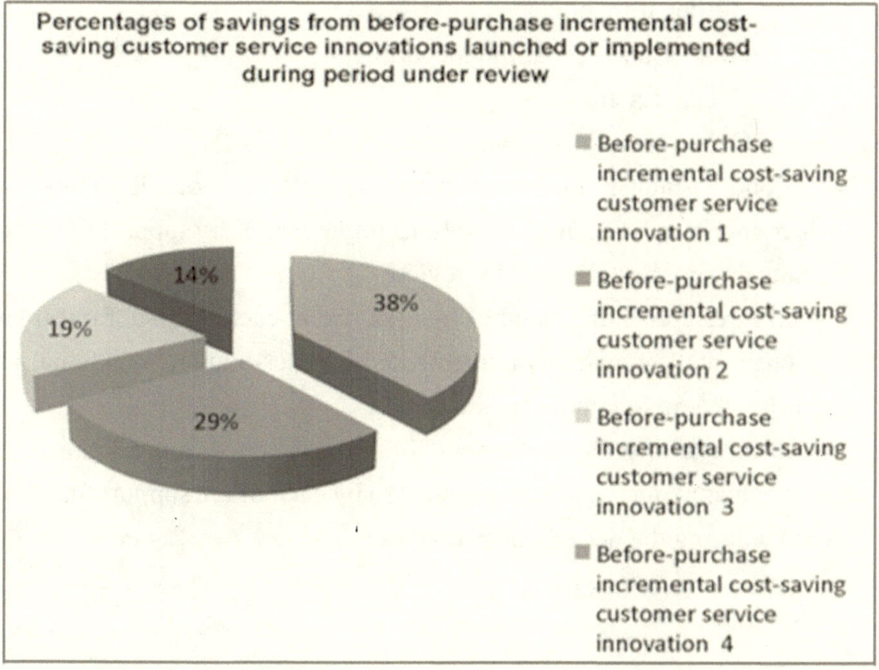

Determining Cost Savings from Innovations Implemented in Support Functional Units

Recall that innovation ideas implemented in support functional units (back-office) are normally radical or incremental cost saving–centered innovations. Thus, this section illustrates how to determine and present cost savings from innovations in support functional units.

Illustration

Assume we'd like to determine the savings gained (in percentage terms) from radical and incremental innovations implemented by the support functional units of DM Personal Care Products between January and December 2021. The five simple steps are as follows:

- First, outline the number of support functional units under consideration. Recall that DM Personal Care Products has the following five support functional units:
    - Procurement department
    - HR department
    - Finance and accounting department
    - IT department
    - Corporate affairs department
- Second, establish the number and types/names of all radical and incremental cost-saving innovations implemented by support functional units during the period under review.
- Third, establish the savings gained from each of the radical and incremental innovations implemented by each support functional unit during the period under review.
- Fourth, establish the total amount of savings gained from all radical and incremental innovations implemented by each of the support functional units during the period under review.

- Fifth, present data showing the percentage of savings gained from each of the radical and incremental innovations implemented by each support functional unit during the period under review.

For illustration purposes, two pie charts present the data: figure 4-49 shows the percentage of cost savings gained from radical innovations by each support functional unit during the period under review, and figure 15-50 shows the percentage of cost savings gained from incremental innovations by each support functional unit in the period under review.

Figure 4-49

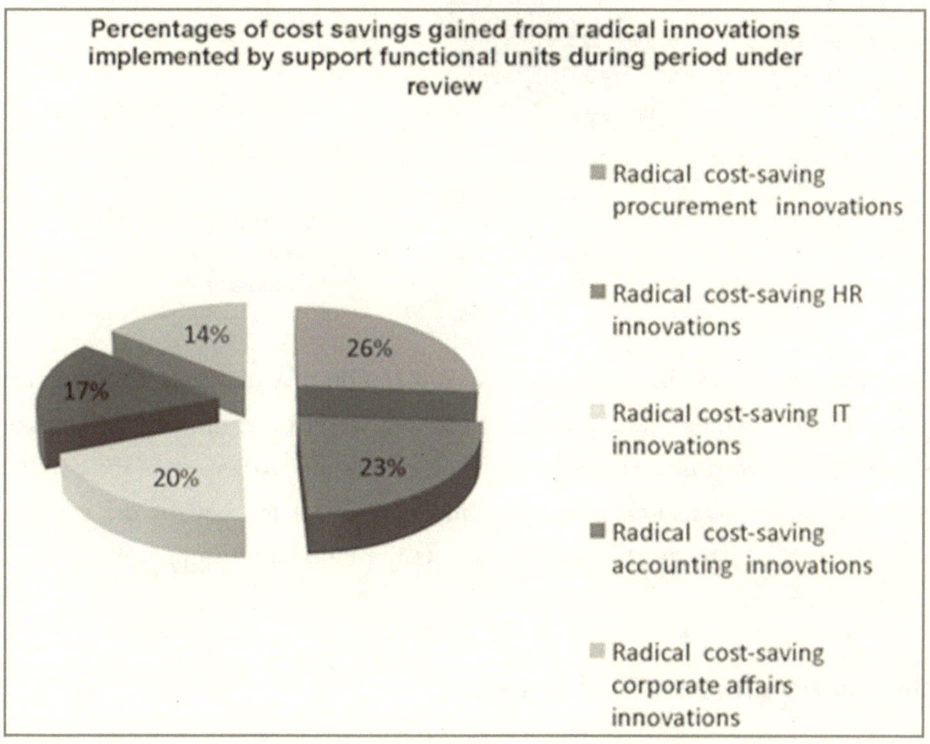

Figure 4-50

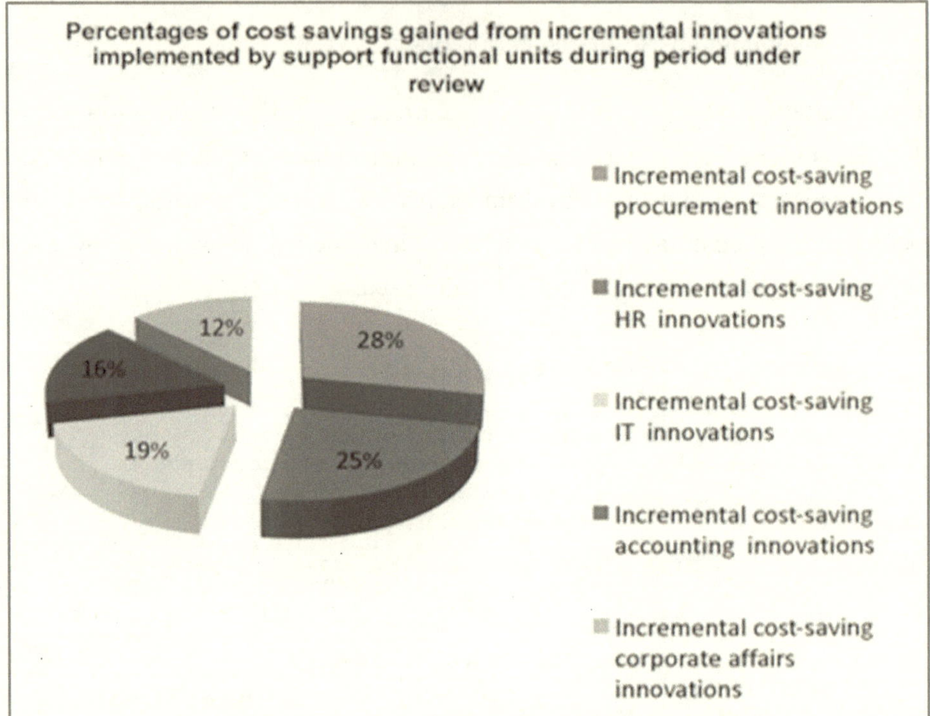

This concludes the discussion and illustration of what innovation impact measurement entails. Recall that in the sections on the other three dimensions of innovation-performance measurement, an evaluation worksheet in the context of each of the measurement approaches appears at the end of the section. Similarly, the last aspect of this section is the innovation impact evaluation, described next.

Innovation Impact Evaluation

As with evaluations of the other three innovation-performance dimensions, the purpose of the innovation impact evaluation is to determine whether the revenue targets or goals from innovations launched or savings gained from cost-saving innovations implemented across functional units were achieved and provide an explanation of why the targets were achieved or missed.

Illustration

For our continuing example of DM Personal Care Products, the innovation impact evaluation is based on the following two aspects:

- Whether the revenue targets or goals from innovations launched or implemented in the core functional units of DM Personal Care Products during the period under review were achieved
- Whether the targets or goals of savings from cost-saving innovations implemented during the period under review were achieved

For illustration purposes, the *innovation impact evaluation worksheet* is applied to three functional units: the product-development unit (Table 4-16), the marketing department (Table 4-17), and the procurement department (Table 4-18).

Table 4-16. Example of Evaluating Impact of Product Innovations

<table>
<tr><td colspan="5">Name of Department: Product-development unit
Date: April 30, 2021</td></tr>
<tr><td colspan="5">Purpose of Evaluation: To assess whether the target or goal of generating a particular amount of revenue from various radical and incremental product innovations launched during the period under review (e.g., January–December of 2021) was achieved

The worksheet is divided into four product categories according to the product segments of the product-development department of DM Personal Care Products:
• Part A: Body-lotions segment
• Part B: Skin-cleansing segment
• Part C: Hair-care segment
• Part D: Hand-washing segment</td></tr>
<tr><td colspan="5">Part A

Percentage of revenue generated from radical and incremental product innovations launched in the body-lotions segment during the period under review</td></tr>
<tr><td colspan="5">Radical: Percentage of revenue generated from radical innovations launched during the period under review</td></tr>
<tr><td rowspan="2">Was the target for this product category achieved? (check "Yes" or "No")</td><td>Yes</td><td>Comment</td><td>No</td><td>Comment</td></tr>
<tr><td></td><td>If yes, indicate the percentage achieved.

Reasons: What factors are responsible for achieving or exceeding the set target?</td><td></td><td>If no, by what percentage was the target missed?

Reasons: What factors are responsible for not meeting the projected target?</td></tr>
</table>

table continues on next page

<table>
<tr><td colspan="5">Incremental: Percentage of revenue generated from incremental innovations launched during the period under review</td></tr>
<tr><td rowspan="2">Was the target for this product category achieved? (check “Yes” or “No”)</td><td>Yes</td><td>Comment</td><td>No</td><td>Comment</td></tr>
<tr><td></td><td>If yes, indicate the percentage achieved.
Reasons: What factors are responsible for achieving or exceeding the set target?</td><td></td><td>If no, by what percentage was the target missed?
Reasons: What factors are responsible for not meeting the projected target?</td></tr>
<tr><td colspan="5">Part B
Percentage of revenue generated from radical and incremental product innovations launched in the skin-cleansing segment</td></tr>
<tr><td colspan="5">Radical: Percentage of revenue generated from radical innovations launched during the period under review</td></tr>
<tr><td rowspan="2">Was the target for this product category achieved? (check “Yes” or “No”)</td><td>Yes</td><td>Comment</td><td>No</td><td>Comment</td></tr>
<tr><td></td><td>If yes, indicate the percentage achieved.
Reasons: What factors are responsible for achieving or exceeding the set target?</td><td></td><td>If no, by what percentage was the target missed?
Reasons: What factors are responsible for not meeting the projected target?</td></tr>
</table>

table continues on next page

<table>
<tr><td colspan="5">Incremental: Percentage of revenue generated from incremental innovations launched during the period under review</td></tr>
<tr><td rowspan="2">Was the target for this product category achieved? (check “Yes” or “No”)</td><td>Yes</td><td>Comment</td><td>No</td><td>Comment</td></tr>
<tr><td></td><td>If yes, indicate the percentage achieved.
Reasons: What factors are responsible for achieving or exceeding the set target?</td><td></td><td>If no, by what percentage was the target missed?
Reasons: What factors are responsible for not meeting the projected target?</td></tr>
<tr><td colspan="5">Part C
Percentage of revenue generated from radical and incremental product innovations launched in the hair-care segment</td></tr>
<tr><td colspan="5">Radical: Percentage of revenue generated from radical innovations launched during the period under review</td></tr>
<tr><td rowspan="2">Was the target for this product category achieved? (check “Yes” or “No”)</td><td>Yes</td><td>Comment</td><td>No</td><td>Comment</td></tr>
<tr><td></td><td>If yes, indicate the percentage achieved.
Reasons: What factors are responsible for achieving or exceeding the set target?</td><td></td><td>If no, by what percentage was the target missed?
Reasons: What factors are responsible for not meeting the projected target?</td></tr>
</table>

table continues on next page

Incremental: **Percentage of revenue generated from incremental innovations launched during the period under review**				
Was the target for this product category achieved? (check "Yes" or "No")	**Yes**	**Comment**	**No**	**Comment**
		If yes, indicate the percentage achieved. **Reasons:** *What factors are responsible for achieving or exceeding the set target?*		If no, by what percentage was the target missed? **Reasons:** *What factors are responsible for not meeting the projected target?*
Part D **Percentage of revenue generated from *radical* and *incremental* product innovation ideas generated in the hand-washing segment**				
Radical: **Percentage of revenue generated from radical innovations launched during the period under review**				
Was the target for this product category achieved? (check "Yes" or "No")	**Yes**	**Comment**	**No**	**Comment**
		If yes, indicate the percentage achieved. **Reasons:** *What factors are responsible for achieving or exceeding the set target?*		If no, by what percentage was the target missed? **Reasons:** *What factors are responsible for not meeting the projected target?*

table continues on next page

<table>
<tr><td colspan="5">Incremental: Percentage of revenue generated from incremental innovations launched during the period under review</td></tr>
<tr><td rowspan="2">Was the target for this product category achieved? (check “Yes” or “No”)</td><td>Yes</td><td>Comment</td><td>No</td><td>Comment</td></tr>
<tr><td></td><td>If yes, indicate the percentage achieved.
Reasons: What factors are responsible for achieving or exceeding the set target?</td><td></td><td>If no, by what percentage was the target missed?
Reasons: What factors are responsible for not meeting the projected target?</td></tr>
</table>

Table 4-17. Example of Evaluating Impact of Marketing Innovations

<table>
<tr><td colspan="5">Name of Department: Marketing department

Date: December 30, 2021</td></tr>
<tr><td colspan="5">Purpose of evaluation: To assess whether the target or goal of generating a particular amount of revenue from various radical and incremental marketing innovations launched during the period under review (e.g., January–December of 2021) was achieved

The worksheet is divided according to the number of subunits or segments of the marketing department of DM Personal Care Products, as follows:

• Part A: Product delivery—two parts: part A (i) for determining revenues generated and part A (ii) for determining savings gained
• Part B: Pricing
• Part C: Product promotion—two parts: part C (i) for determining revenues generated and part C (ii) for determining savings gained
• Part D: New markets
• Part E: Packaging—two parts: part E (i) for determining revenues generated and part E (ii) for determining savings gained</td></tr>
<tr><td colspan="5">Part A (i)

Product delivery (revenues generated)</td></tr>
<tr><td colspan="5">Percentage of revenues generated from radical and incremental innovative methods of delivering products to customers</td></tr>
<tr><td colspan="5">Radical: Percentage of revenues generated from radical innovative methods of delivering products to customers during the period under review</td></tr>
<tr><td rowspan="2">Was the target for this category achieved? (check “Yes” or “No”)</td><td>Yes</td><td>Comment</td><td>No</td><td>Comment</td></tr>
<tr><td></td><td>If yes, indicate the percentage achieved.

Reasons: What factors are responsible for achieving or exceeding the set target?</td><td></td><td>If no, by what percentage was the target missed?

Reasons: What factors are responsible for not meeting the projected target?</td></tr>
</table>

table continues on next page

<table>
<tr><td colspan="5">Incremental: Percentage of revenues generated from incremental innovative methods of delivering products to customers during the period under review</td></tr>
<tr><td rowspan="2">Was the target for this category achieved? (check "Yes" or "No")</td><td>Yes</td><td>Comment</td><td>No</td><td>Comment</td></tr>
<tr><td></td><td>If yes, indicate the percentage achieved.
Reasons: What factors are responsible for achieving or exceeding the set target?</td><td></td><td>If no, by what percentage was the target missed?
Reasons: What factors are responsible for not meeting the projected target?</td></tr>
<tr><td colspan="5">Part A (ii)
Product delivery (savings gained)</td></tr>
<tr><td colspan="5">Percentage of cost savings gained from radical and incremental innovative methods of delivering products to customers during the period under review</td></tr>
<tr><td colspan="5">Radical: Percentage of cost savings made from radical innovative methods of delivering products to customers during the period under review</td></tr>
<tr><td rowspan="2">Was the target for this category achieved? (check "Yes" or "No")</td><td>Yes</td><td>Comment</td><td>No</td><td>Comment</td></tr>
<tr><td></td><td>If yes, indicate the percentage achieved.
Reasons: What factors are responsible for achieving or exceeding the set target?</td><td></td><td>If no, by what percentage was the target missed?
Reasons: What factors are responsible for not meeting the projected target?</td></tr>
</table>

table continues on next page

Incremental: **Percentage of cost savings made from incremental innovative methods of delivering products to customers during the period under review**				
Was the target for this category achieved? (check "Yes" or "No")	**Yes**	**Comment**	**No**	**Comment**
		If yes, indicate the percentage achieved. **Reasons:** *What factors are responsible for achieving or exceeding the set target?*		If no, by what percentage was the target missed? **Reasons:** *What factors are responsible for not meeting the projected target?*
Part B **Product pricing**				
Percentage of revenue generated from *radical* and *incremental* pricing innovations for existing products during the period under review				
Radical: **Percentage of revenue generated from radical pricing innovations on existing products during the period under review**				
Was the target for this category achieved? (check "Yes" or "No")	**Yes**	**Comment**	**No**	**Comment**
		If yes, indicate the percentage achieved. **Reasons:** *What factors are responsible for achieving or exceeding the set target?*		If no, by what percentage was the target missed? **Reasons:** *What factors are responsible for not meeting the projected target?*

table continues on next page

<table>
<tr><td colspan="5">Incremental: Percentage of revenue generated from incremental pricing innovations for existing products during the period under review</td></tr>
<tr><td rowspan="2">Was the target for this category achieved? (check "Yes" or "No")</td><td>Yes</td><td>Comment</td><td>No</td><td>Comment</td></tr>
<tr><td></td><td>If yes, indicate the percentage achieved.
Reasons: What factors are responsible for achieving or exceeding the set target?</td><td></td><td>If no, by what percentage was the target missed?
Reasons: What factors are responsible for not meeting the projected target?</td></tr>
<tr><td colspan="5">Part C (i)
Product promotion (revenue generated)</td></tr>
<tr><td colspan="5">Percentage of revenue generated from radical and incremental product-promotion innovations for existing products during the period under review</td></tr>
<tr><td colspan="5">Radical: Percentage of revenue generated from radical product-promotion innovations for existing products during the period under review</td></tr>
<tr><td rowspan="2">Was the target for this category achieved? (check "Yes" or "No")</td><td>Yes</td><td>Comment</td><td>No</td><td>Comment</td></tr>
<tr><td></td><td>If yes, indicate the percentage achieved.
Reasons: What factors are responsible for achieving or exceeding the set target?</td><td></td><td>If no, by what percentage was the target missed?
Reasons: What factors are responsible for not meeting the projected target?</td></tr>
</table>

table continues on next page

<table>
<tr><td colspan="5">Incremental: Percentage of revenue generated from incremental product-promotion innovations for existing products during the period under review</td></tr>
<tr><td rowspan="2">Was the target for this category achieved? (check “Yes” or “No”)</td><td>Yes</td><td>Comment</td><td>No</td><td>Comment</td></tr>
<tr><td></td><td>If yes, indicate the percentage achieved.
Reasons: What factors are responsible for achieving or exceeding the set target?</td><td></td><td>If no, by what percentage was the target missed?
Reasons: What factors are responsible for not meeting the projected target?</td></tr>
<tr><td colspan="5">Part C (ii)
Product promotion (savings made)</td></tr>
<tr><td colspan="5">Percentage of savings made from radical and incremental product-promotion innovations for existing products during the period under review</td></tr>
<tr><td colspan="5">Radical: Percentage of savings made from radical product-promotion innovations for existing products during the period under review</td></tr>
<tr><td rowspan="2">Was the target for this category achieved? (check “Yes” or “No”)</td><td>Yes</td><td>Comment</td><td>No</td><td>Comment</td></tr>
<tr><td></td><td>If yes, indicate the percentage achieved.
Reasons: What factors are responsible for achieving or exceeding the set target?</td><td></td><td>If no, by what percentage was the target missed?
Reasons: What factors are responsible for not meeting the projected target?</td></tr>
</table>

table continues on next page

<table>
<tr><td colspan="5">Incremental: Percentage of savings made from incremental product-promotion innovations for existing products during the period under review</td></tr>
<tr><td rowspan="2">Was the target for this category achieved? (check "Yes" or "No")</td><td>Yes</td><td>Comment</td><td>No</td><td>Comment</td></tr>
<tr><td></td><td>If yes, indicate the percentage achieved.
Reasons: What factors are responsible for achieving or exceeding the set target?</td><td></td><td>If no, by what percentage was the target missed?
Reasons: What factors are responsible for not meeting the projected target?</td></tr>
<tr><td colspan="5">Part D
New markets (new unserved markets and new-market segments)</td></tr>
<tr><td colspan="5">Revenues from new unserved markets and new-market segments for existing products during the period under review</td></tr>
<tr><td colspan="5">New unserved markets: Percentage of revenues generated from existing products in new unserved markets during the period under review</td></tr>
<tr><td rowspan="2">Was the target for this category achieved? (check "Yes" or "No")</td><td>Yes</td><td>Comment</td><td>No</td><td>Comment</td></tr>
<tr><td></td><td>If yes, indicate the percentage achieved.
Reasons: What factors are responsible for achieving or exceeding the set target?</td><td></td><td>If no, by what percentage was the target missed?
Reasons: What factors are responsible for not meeting the projected target?</td></tr>
</table>

table continues on next page

<table>
<tr><td colspan="5">New-market segments: Percentage of revenues generated from existing products in new-market segments during the period under review</td></tr>
<tr><td rowspan="2">Was the target for this category achieved? (check "Yes" or "No")</td><td>Yes</td><td>Comment</td><td>No</td><td>Comment</td></tr>
<tr><td></td><td>If yes, indicate the percentage achieved.
Reasons: What factors are responsible for achieving or exceeding the set target?</td><td></td><td>If no, by what percentage was the target missed?
Reasons: What factors are responsible for not meeting the projected target?</td></tr>
<tr><td colspan="5">Part E (i)
Packaging (revenues generated)</td></tr>
<tr><td colspan="5">Percentage of revenues generated from radical and incremental packaging innovations launched during the period under review</td></tr>
<tr><td colspan="5">Radical: Percentage of revenues generated from radical packaging innovations launched during the period under review</td></tr>
<tr><td rowspan="2">Was the target for this category achieved? (check "Yes" or "No")</td><td>Yes</td><td>Comment</td><td>No</td><td>Comment</td></tr>
<tr><td></td><td>If yes, indicate the percentage achieved.
Reasons: What factors are responsible for achieving or exceeding the set target?</td><td></td><td>If no, by what percentage was the target missed?
Reasons: What factors are responsible for not meeting the projected target?</td></tr>
</table>

table continues on next page

<table>
<tr><td colspan="5">Incremental: Percentage of revenues generated from incremental packaging innovations launched during the period under review</td></tr>
<tr><td rowspan="2">Was the target for this category achieved? (check "Yes" or "No")</td><td>Yes</td><td>Comment</td><td>No</td><td>Comment</td></tr>
<tr><td></td><td>If yes, indicate the percentage achieved.
Reasons: What factors are responsible for achieving or exceeding the set target?</td><td></td><td>If no, by what percentage was the target missed?
Reasons: What factors are responsible for not meeting the projected target?</td></tr>
<tr><td colspan="5">Part E (ii)
Packaging (savings made)</td></tr>
<tr><td colspan="5">Percentage of cost savings gained from radical and incremental packaging innovations launched during the period under review</td></tr>
<tr><td colspan="5">Radical: Percentage of cost savings gained from radical packaging innovations launched during the period under review</td></tr>
<tr><td rowspan="2">Was the target for this category achieved? (check "Yes" or "No")</td><td>Yes</td><td>Comment</td><td>No</td><td>Comment</td></tr>
<tr><td></td><td>If yes, indicate the percentage achieved.
Reasons: What factors are responsible for achieving or exceeding the set target?</td><td></td><td>If no, by what percentage was the target missed?
Reasons: What factors are responsible for not meeting the projected target?</td></tr>
</table>

table continues on next page

<table>
<tr><td colspan="5">Incremental: Percentage of cost savings gained from incremental packaging innovations launched during the period under review</td></tr>
<tr><td rowspan="2">Was the target for this category achieved? (check “Yes” or “No”)</td><td>Yes</td><td>Comment</td><td>No</td><td>Comment</td></tr>
<tr><td></td><td>If yes, indicate the percentage achieved.
Reasons: What factors are responsible for achieving or exceeding the set target?</td><td></td><td>If no, by what percentage was the target missed?
Reasons: What factors are responsible for not meeting the projected target?</td></tr>
</table>

Worksheets 4-15 and 4-16 show how the evaluation worksheet can be applied to two different core functional units (product development and marketing). Similarly, the evaluation worksheet can be applied to the other core functional units of DM Personal Care Products:

- Manufacturing-processes department
- Customer service department

Table 4-18 shows how the evaluation worksheet can be applied to the support functional units of DM Personal Care Products, using the procurement department as an example.

Table 4-18. Example of Evaluating Impact of Cost-Saving Procurement Innovations

<table>
<tr><td colspan="5">Name of Department: Procurement department

Date: December 30, 2021</td></tr>
<tr><td colspan="5">Purpose of evaluation: To assess whether the target or goal of gaining a particular amount of savings from various radical and incremental procurement innovations implemented during the period under review (e.g., January–December of 2021) was achieved

The worksheet is divided into two parts, as follows:
• Part A: Percentage of savings gained from radical procurement innovations implemented during the period under review
• Part B: Percentage of savings gained from incremental procurement innovations implemented during the period under review</td></tr>
<tr><td colspan="5" align="center">Part A

Percentage of savings gained from radical procurement innovations implemented during the period under review</td></tr>
<tr><td rowspan="2">Was the target for this category achieved? (check "Yes" or "No")</td><td>Yes</td><td>Comment</td><td>No</td><td>Comment</td></tr>
<tr><td></td><td>If yes, indicate the percentage achieved.

Reasons: What factors are responsible for achieving or exceeding the set target?</td><td></td><td>If no, by what percentage was the target missed?

Reasons: What factors are responsible for not meeting the projected target?</td></tr>
</table>

table continues on next page

<table>
<tr><th colspan="5">Part B
Percentage of savings gained from incremental procurement innovations implemented during the period under review</th></tr>
<tr><td rowspan="2">Was the target for this category achieved? (check "Yes" or "No")</td><td>Yes</td><td>Comment</td><td>No</td><td>Comment</td></tr>
<tr><td></td><td>If yes, indicate the percentage achieved.
Reasons: What factors are responsible for achieving or exceeding the set target?</td><td></td><td>If no, by what percentage was the target missed?
Reasons: What factors are responsible for not meeting the projected target?</td></tr>
</table>

Similar evaluation worksheets would be created for the other four support functional units of DM Personal Care Products:

- HR department
- Finance and accounting department
- IT department
- Corporate affairs department

Tables 4-16 through 4-18 show how the evaluation worksheet can be applied to determine whether the goals for target revenue and cost savings from innovations launched or implemented during the period under review were achieved and the reasons why they were met or missed.

Bottom line

There are three takeaways from Part I. First, you cannot sustain a culture of innovation without an effective mechanism for tracking and measuring innovation performance across functional units of the company. Second, many companies face difficulties in measuring and reporting the innovation performance across functional units. Third, Part I has suggested metrics and tools to help organizational leaders build essential skills and knowledge for measuring and reporting innovation performance across functional units.

Part II

HOW TO STRUCTURE THE REPORT

Overview

In the introduction section, we stated that the purpose of the book is to create a mechanism for measuring and reporting innovation performance in companies. To achieve this, the book is structured in two parts. Part I covered five main sections, the introduction, steps one, two, three and four. Part II covers some the vital aspects to consider when structuring an innovation performance report. They include: (1) introduction by the CEO, (2) executive summary, and (3) presentation format.

1. Introduction by the CEO

This section should have sentiments by the CEO. Here are some the things that could be highlighted:

- The CEO's emotional interest and passion for creating a culture of innovation and how measuring and reporting innovation performance of all functional units contributes to the aspiration of making the company an innovation-led.

- Articulate why innovation is critical to sustainable competitiveness and growth and realizing the company vision.
- Why it is important for the company to implement a company-wide mechanism for measuring and reporting innovation performance.
- The CEO must reiterate the company's desire to make every functional unit and employee responsible for innovation.

2. Executive Summary

The executive summary of the innovation performance report should highlight the purpose in relation to the innovation aspirations of functional units and the organization as a whole. So, the statements should be simple and clear. That being said, much of the information in this section must focus on outlining corporate innovation and innovation goals of all the functional units.

3. Presentation Format

As suggested by the subtitle, this section should highlight two things: (i) the metrics adopted and (ii) the presentation style of the innovation performance-related data provided in the report.

i. *Metrics used*

   Describe in the context of each metric and how it has been applied to interpret innovation performance of each functional and the entire organization.

   Remember the four metric-approach used in this book? That is:

   - Innovation input measurement
   - Innovation output measurement
   - Innovation-results measurement
   - Innovation impact measurement

ii. *Presentation style*

   Outline in brief the presentation style used for each innovation performance metric. For example, could be tables, charts, or graphs.

Whatever presentation style you choose to use, it must be simple and easy to understand by all the workforces.

Bottom line

There are three takeaways from Part I. First, organizational leaders face difficulties when it comes what metrics to adopt or use for reporting innovation performance. Second, Part II has suggested metrics and presentational styles for presenting innovation performance-related data.

SUMMARY

Let's recap the five main aspects the book has covered:

1. You cannot sustain a culture of innovation without an effective mechanism for tracking and measuring innovation performance across functional units of the company.
2. Many companies face difficulties in measuring and reporting the innovation performance across functional units.
3. The book has suggested four metrics for measuring innovation performance across functional units.
4. Metrics and tools to help organizational leaders build essential skills and knowledge for measuring and reporting innovation performance across functional units.
5. Some presentational styles for communicating innovation performance-related data.

SELECTED REFERENCES

1. Dr. Edwin A. Locke, Towards a theory of task motivation and incentives, *Journal of Organizational Behavior and Human Performance, 1968, Volume 3, Issue 2*
2. David Masumba, *Leadership for Innovation (2020)*
3. How to measure innovation" How to Measure Innovation https://www.fastcompany.com/3031788/how-to-measure-innovation-to-get-real-results
4. "Measuring Innovation " *https://www.bcg.com/documents/file15484.pdf*
5. The CFO's Role in Fostering Innovation*" http://deloitte.wsj.com/cfo/2015/08/12/the-cfos-role-in-fostering-innovation/*

www.ingramcontent.com/pod-product-compliance
Lightning Source LLC
LaVergne TN
LVHW050957080826
845145LV00009B/2334

* 9 7 8 1 7 3 4 1 9 1 3 7 0 *